Advanced Kindle Book Marketing:

How to Sell more Ebooks online with new Amazon promotions and Kindle Bestseller tips

By Award-Winning and Bestselling Authors Lucinda Sue Crosby and Laura Dobbins

LuckyCinda
USA

ISBN: 978-0-9960898-9-0

Printed in the US

LuckyCinda
www.luckycinda.com
laura@luckycinda.com

Book Design: Laura Dobbins

Disclaimer

There are no guarantees that you will make any money using the ideas and tips within this book. Since it is so dependent on genre, customer wants and your own marketing plans, how many books you sell cannot be specified. But if you work hard and apply these methods, you should see some profit increase with your books.

This book is not associated with or endorsed by Amazon, CreateSpace or Kindle Direct Publishing.

Table of Contents

FOREWORD: 9

PART I: Reviewing the basics:
How to write, publish and design a book

Chapter 1: Planning Ahead 14

Chapter 2: Selling Strategies – Create a Marketing Plan.. 20

Chapter 3: Marketing techniques: – Keywords, Categories, Book Descriptions, Online publicity................................. 25

Chapter 4: Sell more Kindle Books using proper keywords 35

Chapter 5: The Right Book Categories help you Sell Books 48

Chapter 6: How to create book descriptions that convert into sales... 53

Chapter 7: Take advantage of Amazon – your best book publicity tool 59

Part II: Marketing, Marketing, Marketing:
Free Days, Book Reviews, Social Media and other publicity ideas

Chapter 8: How to Navigate KDP Select – Use your Free Days Strategically 65

Chapter 9: Kindle Matchbook, Kindle Countdown Promos and $.99 Kindle Deals.. 86

Chapter 10: Book Reviews – how to get your book into the right hands.. 100

Chapter 11: Social Media and other promo opportunities 107

Bonus Chapter and Author Resources:

Chapter 12: BONUS CHAPTER - Looking ahead......... 134

Dear readers:.. 147

About the Authors: 149

Reference Page: Author Tools 152

Author Programs we recommend: 159

Amazon programs that also help promote your books: .. 161

Site links for your Kindle Promotions:

KDP and places to list Free Day Promotions: 162

Kindle Countdown and places to list Promotions:.......... 168

.99 Kindle Deals and places to list Promotions: 172

List of our other books all available at AMAZON:........ 175

Advanced Kindle Book Marketing

How to sell more Ebooks online
with new Amazon promotions and
Kindle Bestseller tips

FOREWORD:

You've written a great novel. No reason it shouldn't be a bestseller – at least according to your family and friends. So why is it, once published and sitting on the world's biggest online retailer's site, no one is buying it? The simple answer: No one is aware of your book EXCEPT your family and friends. This begs the question: Is there a remedy for obscurity?

YES!!!

There are many legitimate ebook marketing strategies but some are confusing. If you are not tech-savvy, the machinations required to get your book noticed can seem overwhelming. But if you master the concepts in the following chapters, you will sell more books. To assist you, we have written this guide as a step-by-step instruction kit to help you navigate your promotional efforts and included the latest marketing opportunities for 2014-2015.

Here's a look at some of our topics:

New marketing opportunities on Amazon

Selling more Kindle Books through keywords

Using built-in Amazon promotion tools to reach readers

Marketing, Marketing, Marketing

Partnering up – A list of websites that will boost your promotion efforts

BONUS CHAPTER – Advance marketing techniques

While the focus of this book is selling on Amazon, many of these formulas will help you at other retail sites. If you apply what you learn, your book sales should increase. Of course, we can't promise you Bestseller status but we can show you how to make real progress, as we have.

Here's to your success and feel free to visit our website for free and paid book promotions:

http://kindlebookpromos.luckycinda.com

Part I

Reviewing the basics:

How to write, publish and design a book

Chapter 1: Planning Ahead

Yes, you've heard it a 100 times but it is STILL worth repeating – the necessities for "Bestseller" status are: Title, Content, Design and Selling Strategy.

Let's take a closer look at each step.

Title – When possible use names and phrases people are searching

There was a time when catchy titles or great cover art were enough. In today's digital market, with more than 2.2 million books available, consumers need even more of an impetus to become interested in your product. Therefore, choosing a title and chapter headings that incorporate the same phrases your target readers are searching online will make it easier for them to spot and identify with your product. Subtitles are another smart way to let people know in a few words what the book has to offer or what the story is about.

We admit this is easier to accomplish in nonfiction but it's not impossible with fiction and certainly worthwhile. For example we published an ebook marketing guide we titled: *Sell more Ebooks – How to increase sales and Amazon rankings using Kindle Direct Publishing.*

- There are 4 key phrases in this heading that readers – mostly other authors in this case – search for on Google and Amazon: "Sell more Ebooks," "How to increase sales," How to increase Amazon rankings," and "Kindle Direct Publishing."
- The reader gets a sense of what the book is about

When we published our prize-winning romance adventure, *Francesca of Lost Nation,* we were not familiar with the importance of keywords and titles. If we had been, we'd have realized that most people wouldn't be searching the words,

"Francesca," or "Lost Nation," when seeking books. For us, a subtitle was the easy fix: *Francesca of Lost Nation – an Old-Fashioned Romance Suspense.*

- "Old fashion," "romance" and "suspense" are popular genres
- Even people who stumble upon our title will get an idea what the book is about by the subhead while those specifically looking for an old-fashion romance and/or suspense will also be targeted.

Other tips for choosing a compelling title:

- Keep your title as short as possible and to the point
- One-line phrases work beautifully. What is your book really about? Synthesize your answer into a tight group of words that would grab your attention, make you curious and entice you to investigate further.

Content – Determine what you want to Communicate and Why

Authors write either fiction or non-fiction with a rare few able to produce both. Your thought process will differ slightly depending on your writing intentions. For example, a memoir's intention may be to share personal lessons with others who have had similar experiences. Conversely, a personal story may be written as a recorded history for family and friends. Can you see how intention determines your target audience and your marketing strategies to reach specific consumers?

If fiction is your specialty, you'll want to reach out to enthusiasts of that genre. And even within these categories you can tighten your niche. Is your romance novel erotic, old fashioned or general? The more you can narrow your description groups, the easier it will become to sell your product.

It's a safe bet that most authors and publishers of the 2.2 million digital books and the 22 million or more in print on Amazon would be attracted to books about book marketing So, how-to guides about e-promotion, book selling, online marketing or other 21st century advertising methods have a high potential to be bestsellers in these categories. Other current specialty topics like Health, Food or Home Business are building followers.

Regarding fiction trends, series are popular now. If you can build a loyal fan base with a good first book in a series of three or five titles, you'll earn superior returns on your investment. It (almost) goes without saying that romance in all forms and mystery suspense continue to outsell most other categories.

Tips:
- Explore your particular niche by checking out what's hot at online book retailers or at your local book store ... Investigate what topics continuously make the bestseller lists. Keep a desktop folder of your findings – the info will come in handy later on.

- Write what you know –
  a. Are you a web designer? You can write a variety of books on this topic like: How to use basic html to make your website pop; Web Design made easy; Best Templates for Web Building ... and the list goes on.

  b. Writing fiction? If you're lucky, you'll have quirky, dashing or infamous relatives with fascinating backgrounds you can feature as main or title chaacters. Uuse their stories, mannerisms, relationships and life experiences and then embellish a little or a lot – but don't skimp on accuracy of time, place and setting. Paying attention to historical and geographical details will help lure your reader into the universe you have created.

Content – Quality matters
  a. **Professional Editing:** If you want to secure buyers and keep them coming back for more, make sure their experience with your manuscript is a pristine one. Present error-free copy with professional quality content and copy editing, design and formatting.

16

Accidental grammar errors, misplaced punctuation, and unintentionally misspelled words will all bounce a reader right out of the text, no matter how poetic or life-altering. The money you spend on professional help – an editor, a copy editor and a proof reader – is the soundest investment you can make in your product.

Design – Looking GOOD!

First impressions matter to consumers, even more so online than on a book shelf at a store, because you can rarely scan or read through a book online.

Following are some suggestions for good cover designs excerpted from our book, *Sell more Ebooks – How to increase sales and Amazon rankings using Kindle Direct Publishing:*

Invoke an emotional response with eye-grabbing ideas

a. Believe it or not, less IS more.
Keep it clean and leave plenty of "white space" (empty area). Try to avoid too much fancy artwork or complicated designs that detract from the title or main thrust of the cover art and make sure your fonts can be easily read!
What type of covers pique your interest? Look at books in your genre – and in your personal library – to see what styles or layouts appeal to you most.

b. Mood Indigo - Setting the stage:
The colors and images you use should evoke feelings/impressions in potential buyers. Determine what type of reaction you are seeking and do some research on how to produce that reaction visually.
USA Today took some jabs from design dilettantes and journalism traditionalists on the launch of its newspaper in 1982. Today the Gannet-owned publication is one of the most widely circulated newspapers in the United States, boasting a 1.8 million readership as of March 2012.

USA Today divides its newspaper sections by colors. It uses an easy to read set-up, dozens of images per edition as well as graphics and maps throughout the publication.

Many newspapers across the country carry the same news ... some even employ the same photos and maps. But few have enticed readers the way *USA Today* has done with its innovative presentation.

c. Is a picture worth 1,000 words? Artwork is crucial.

Your cover is the potential buyer's first introduction to your labor of love and its content.

- Bottom line: Don't use an image that distorts the first impression of your story or one that doesn't set the tone properly for what's inside. If possible, pay for a professional to do the work. It costs $349 for a custom cover at Amazon's Createspace.com.
- The Small Publishers, Artists and Writers Network (SPAWN) offers a $100 book design discount to its members for services at: http://www.logicalexpressions.com/

There are reasonably priced and knowledgeable freelance artists. Most professionals host or have access to a web site that carries examples of covers they've created. You'll have to do some nosing around and you might query on-line author forums.

- John Kremer, book marketing expert and bestselling author, has an extensive list of artists at his website: http://www.bookmarket.com/101des.htm.

But if you need to or wish to design the covers yourself, look for royalty-free art or pay someone up front for their photos or graphics. It's less complicated to buy these components outright so you don't have to deal with copyright or use issues later on.

- We recommend http://www.flickr.com/creativecommons/org and www.clipart.com when building your own covers.
- We've also used www.dreamstime.com and Getty Photos.
- Stock.xchng is somewhat limited but all the images are free.

d. You need a backbone! Don't forget the spine.
For those of you that desire both digital and print copies, it's important to remember that when standing upright on a shelf, the spine may be all that's visible to a potential reader. This makes it valuable space. The spine should display your name and book title.

e. Format to E-books
Proper formatting is a must. If you don't do it WELL, pay someone. Amazon provides a long list of ebook converting services: http://bit.ly/19ymFKP.
Fiverr is a great service to seek professional help for $5 but don't just hire the first service you see. Look at the person's rankings, customer remarks and service delivery times.
The easiest method is to create the original text-only document in Microsoft Word and then convert it using free conversion software. Please check out the following sites:
http://ebook.online-convert.com/convert-to-epub
http://www.epubconverter.org/

New for 2014: Amazon KDP Select has added a number of tools in the past few months to aid authors with their book publishing experience. Amazon KDP now offers plugins, ebook conversion tools and epub creator.
http://bit.ly/1dmo7Mj

Chapter 2: Selling Strategies – Create a Marketing Plan

No matter what you publish, you need to have some idea how you will promote it. If you have extra income and can hire an expert, more power to you. However, most writers don't have enough disposable income to go that route - or know who to trust with their labors of love.

So ...

- The basics – Budget, Time, Platforms
- Advanced techniques – Keywords, Categories, Book Descriptions, Online publicity

a. Budget

ISBN: Some initial costs for your book include obtaining an ISBN. Bookstores require an International Standard Book Number (ISBN). This will identify your work's publisher and allow you to sell books to retailers, libraries and bookstores. An ISBN costs $125 each or bundles of 10 for $295. You can also obtain an ISBN for $55 if you are going to sell directly to consumers instead of through stores and libraries.

Note: There are a number of ISBN services available for authors, only some of whom are legitimate. Publisher Services – one of the largest authorized agencies of the US ISBN Agency has a detailed article on the subject: *The Importance of Getting an Authorized and Legitimate ISBN Number.*

Library of Congress/Copyright: Obtaining a Library of Congress number is free but you will have to pay postage to send your finished product and it will cost $45 to secure the actual copyright. Although some printing companies will obtain these numbers for you, you'll still be responsible for processing fees.

Printing: Whether you print your books using Print on Demand (from one to 100 books at a time) or go traditional (in bundles of 200 or more), it will come out of your pocket. If you do plan on selling print versions of your title, remember to include distribution, storage and shipping costs. Frankly, that's what makes POD attractive – no overhead.

Keep in mind that major retailers don't like POD because it generally indicates an INDY author, which is still frowned upon by some of the major players. POD also interferes with traditional buy-back policies, an agreement between publishers, distributors and retailers. For now, let's just keep it simple.

Other costs:

- **Website:** If you plan on having a blog or website, which we highly recommend, you will need to consider domain registration and hosting costs. You can learn more about these online. GoDaddy.com, Hostgator.com and Wordpress.com are three popular sites.

- **Travel:** Some expenses authors often forget to include in their money plans are travel, lodging and food. If you plan on attending book signings, seminars or other events, be sure to allow for line items in your budget.

- **Advertising:** Even if your plan is for digital sales only, you will need to advertise above and beyond posting to your own website. While most advertising on digital book publicity sites is inexpensive, it will add up. NOTE: Most of these fees will cover one-day only ads.

- **Outsourcing:** Article writing and blogging are free but if you don't have the time it takes to manage these functions, you'll want to pay someone to do it. Eventually, you can invest in software that can streamline some of these tasks.

- **Miscellaneous:** Don't forget flyers, business cards, book giveaways, press kits, postage and traditional advertising in print, radio and other media.

As you can see, forging ahead without a plan could be a costly mistake. Thoroughly vetting so-called promotional experts will protect you from investing time and money with people that can't or won't deliver. Do the homework!

b. Time – How much of it do you have?

If you can't hire someone else, allot yourself plenty of time to do it yourself. Here are some items to include in your schedule:

- Sending out press releases
- Blogging
- Setting up online ads
- Setting up and conducting interviews, book signings, public or online appearances and speaking engagements
- Keeping current with orders, emails or phone calls
- Posting to social media – especially during a KDP promotion

d. Platforms

Decide which online forums work best for you. We prefer Facebook, Linkedin and Twitter. Because we have a staff, we also operate three websites. In the beginning, one website and reasonable activity on one social site may be enough.

Each platform has slightly different audiences and forum rules. One great way to navigate is to offer more than you're asking for in return. Really!

- **Facebook** – Many author- and book-friendly sites allow you to post about your book when you're offering your title for free through Kindle Direct Publishing Free Days. Tips:
  a. Post no more often than twice per day during your Free Day promotions and no more than once every week or two when your titles are not free. Be sure to familiarize yourself with site rules and comply with all guidelines.
  b. Don't just promote your books all the time; try to post helpful tips or suggestions for other authors and readers.

    c. Post cool photos or interesting news clips that relate to the site you are visiting. And be sure to "Like" other people's offerings.

- **Linkedin** – Professional blogging forum. Look for topic sites like book marketing, authors of your genre, writing tips, ebook sales and anything that would interest you or topics about which you can offer your own contributions.
  - a. Don't promote unless the topic moderator allows it or it is a group with an expressed interest in your topic.
  - b. Offer helpful information and, when appropriate, you can post links to your site as long as it isn't blatant self-promotion. Become involved for a month or two to get a feel for what is appropriate and what isn't before you promote any of your work. Of course, feel free to answer any query honestly when asked for information.

- **Twitter** – This can be a great tool if used properly. The key is to team up with people who can help you get the word out about your promotions or book titles. Look for book reviewers, bloggers, readers and promoters.
  - a. Twitter profiles usually specify a user's interests and website. We suggest visiting other people's websites to see what they offer. We run Kindle Book Promos (a site that features authors, kindle books and book marketing tips) – so we are always looking for similar sites we can team up with to promote each other's writers, links and products. This creates additional exposure on both sides of the exchange and can expand retweeting exponentially.
  - b. Network with people whose natural fit can help you. Looking for book reviews? Seek out book readers, bloggers or reviewers on Twitter. You

can do that through the search box or the #
Discover link. You can always direct message
fans that follow you back but it is actually less
of a hassle to visit their websites and use their
contact forms or email. This is especially true
when requesting an interview or book review,
which would take more than the 140 characters
allotted for Twitter posts.

c. Use Twitter to promote others more than
yourself and it will come back to you. You can
post frequently on Twitter due to the volume of
posts listed per minute. However, refrain from
posting every second of every day. Caution: if
you post the same message consistently
throughout the day, users will start to block you
and Twitter will suspend your account.

There are other books with greater detail on each of
these social forums. While these are the most popular, there are
several other heavy weight social sites including groups at
Kindle Boards and Amazon. (**See our resource list at the end of
this book**)

Chapter 3: Marketing techniques: – Keywords, Categories, Book Descriptions, Online publicity

Covering the basics is necessary for publishing your work; marketing your masterpiece will require more advanced techniques. It isn't enough to have a great story, book design or appealing product price. Today's authors need to market their work as or even before it's made available to the public. And ideally, you want your book title, description and website to use keywords that will drive traffic to you. Even choosing book categories will determine how people find you.

Keywords and How to Use Them

Potential customers find and purchase products through identifiable and predictable code phrases because that's how internet search engines are designed ... to match a specific request with a specific result. Keywords are powerful tools for assisting internet surfers to find and purchase any product in general and your book in particular. Carefully chosen keywords, therefore, should be included when creating your headlines and book descriptions.

Why is it that authors will happily spend days or even years researching historical content for a novel but won't spend a few minutes researching keywords? If you really grasped how many sales are made simply by choosing the proper terms and phrases for titles and sub-titles, you'd understand it was time worth spent.

BTW, we know excruciatingly well from experience that terms like *keywords, search engine optimization* – or especially the dreaded *algorithms* – can scare the pants off civilians. But familiarizing yourself with these terms and the strategies they represent is a vital step in the process of becoming a successful INDY author.

We promise to make the learning process as painless as possible!

The following information is an in-depth explanation of keywords and how to use them. We also have an easy step-by-step summary for those on data overload. (**See Chapter 4**)

First a brief definition of online marketing terms:

Keywords are words and phrases that describe a product or service. A lengthier explanation might be: keywords are words or phrases relevant to your book's content that online searchers can use to find you. It's like leaving a trail of breadcrumbs for Hansel and Gretel to follow.

If and when you "optimize" these searches, it will be that much easier for purchasers to find you ... which will in turn lead to increased traffic ... which will lead to more book sales ... ergo:

Search Engine Optimization (SEO): a technique used to ensure that your book – or any other product – ranks as high as possible on the search results pages. For example, when you are looking for something on the internet, you use Google or Yahoo or Bing. You describe what you're looking for in your subject box, click the Enter button and scan the posted results. Since studies show that most people are far more likely to select items or links listed on the first page of results, that's where your item needs to be located.

Say you've written a book about bread recipes. Obviously, you should title it so that people looking for bread recipes can easily navigate to your work. The rule might be: Make your titles specific to the pool of potential buyers.

Fiction writers, ditto. In fact, it's becoming common practice for novelists to include a subtitle: *An old-fashioned romance. A light-hearted mystery. A fast-paced thriller.*

Be creative, to the point and target savvy.

Tip: Few self-published authors understand SEO and marketing. But if you learn enough about it to apply it, you'll outsell your competition.

The Nuts and Bolts of Keywords

Search engines operate on three types of software, Spider, Index and Query, that work together to collect, analyze and index web pages. Only after a web surfer enters words or a phrase in the search box is the collective information collated and made available. Over time, marketing gurus can determine which keywords people are using most for any particular product or service.

So what does that mean for authors?

It means you need to find out what people are looking for online and then find a way to position your book on the appropriate "first search pages" of Google and Amazon. If your book is consistently buried on the third page of results or lower, it will be difficult for you to compete. Under ideal circumstances, keyword research should be done prior to writing your book – especially for nonfiction wordsmiths, although fiction writers will benefit from this step too. Amazon and Google are the two largest traffic sites available for authors and once you know how, you'll be able to take advantage of the free assistance both make available.

Try not to feel intimidated! You don't have to become a techno geek; just learn the basics.

Using keywords in your Book Descriptions

Whenever it makes sense, keywords should be incorporated into your book title. While it's not difficult to use traffic-driving terms or phrases in non-fiction headings, you may wish to add a subtitle to plug in necessary wordage for fiction.

As you upload your book to Kindle Direct Publishing, you'll be asked for a book title as well as a subtitle (if you have one).

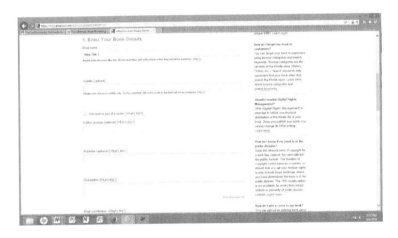

In addition, you'll be allowed seven "descriptive words or phrases – known as keywords" plus a lengthy description. A savvy marketer would include similar keywords and phrases in each of these sections.

Amazon allows for a total of seven one-term and/or multiple term concepts and this is where doing your homework will pay off Big Time. Because these simple "descriptions" will become the building block of the information Amazon uses to promote your book. Amazon will also use them to help readers find your product.

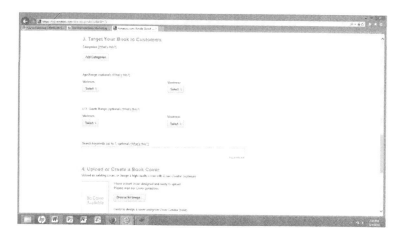

Tip: If you have a book that crosses over into more than one genre, be sure to take advantage of that happy fact in your keywords, tags and title description. A wider outreach ensures a broader customer base.

Keywords should be used on your website or blog, in any press releases or online articles you post and on social media forums you join like Goodreads and Smashwords. Try keeping the content in everyday language so that your information flows naturally.

GREAT TOOL: We are affiliates of The Author Marketing Club and recommend you become a member. The Author Marketing Club has great marketing tools for authors including software that walks you through the Kindle Direct Publishing upload process and formats your content to stand out on Amazon. For details as well as a free e-book on writing better Amazon descriptions, CLICK HERE.

Final Thoughts:

- When writing articles or blog posts, limit yourself to two keywords or phrases per each 100 words.
- For the greatest impact, ensure your descriptions are brief, informative and relevant to your service or product.
- Proof your work exhaustively. It needs to make sense. (Listening to a friend read the copy out loud will be surprisingly helpful.)
- Stay away from generic terms because you want to target potential buyers who are specifically searching for a product like yours. For example, instead of listing your genre as Romance, be more specific: Paranormal Romance.
- Be open to change and adapt as necessary. Experimentation, including trial and failure, are viable parts of this process.

Why descriptions and tags rock

Consider your purchasing habits on Amazon: When browsing the top 100 Kindle books, for example, you may come across a topic that sounds intriguing. If you've never heard the title before or you're not familiar with the author, you'll probably click "Look Inside." If you like what you see, you'll consider ordering and if the book is free, that decision is a no-brainer. But what if the cost is $3.99? Or $7.99?

Now let's say a web surfer/potential customer is attracted to your book on impulse because of a catchy title or a seductive cover. Unless your price is $0.00, that reader will still need to be convinced to invest his or her time and money in your product. That's why your book description is such an important tool in your sales kit: it's often the tipping point that makes or breaks the sale.

Too many authors overlook this important aspect of promotion. They slap together five sentences almost as an afterthought and hope for the best. What a lost opportunity! We hope, after reading this, that you don't make the same mistake.

Main Elements of Description:

Character – Who is the main character and what is she/he trying to accomplish or overcome?

Setting – Where or when does the story take place? What is the genre?

Feelings – How can you appeal to the reader's emotions? To evoke images and mood, use unusual yet relevant adjectives, hyphenated terms, eloquent nouns and action verbs. Take a thriller, for example: Instead of writing, "My book is a Thriller," summarize your story using words or terms like, "terrifying," "hair-raising," "adrenaline-kicking," "goose bump-inducing" or "heart-pounding." Your readers don't need to be told THIS IS A THRILLER; they'll get it from the description.

Karen McQuestion, (www.karenmcquestion.com) is the author of nine books, including a novel that has been optioned for film called, *A Scattered Life.* She offers this illustration of a great book description using "power" words:

Example: *The Da Vinci Code* by Dan Brown

Robert Langdon is a Harvard professor of symbology who can't stay out of trouble. Last seen in Angels and Demons (2000), this mild-mannered academic finds himself entangled in a deadly conspiracy that stretches back centuries. Visiting Paris on business, he is awakened at 2:00 a.m. by a call from the police: An elderly curator has been murdered inside the Louvre, and a baffling cipher has been found near the body. Aided by the victim's cryptologist granddaughter, Langdon begins a danger-filled quest for the culprit; but the deeper he searches, the more he becomes convinced that long-festering conspiracies hold the answer to the art lover's death.

Take a closer look at the words used:

trouble
entangled
deadly conspiracy
elderly curator
murdered
baffling cipher
danger-filled quest
culprit
long-festering conspiracies
death

The ideal book description conveys the genre, summarizes the story and offers enough insight into the characters to intrigue the reader.

From the above example, we know Robert Langdon is a Harvard professor of symbology who can't stay out of trouble; that he is on a danger-filled quest; and that the story takes place in Paris. The description isn't too short nor does it give the plot away.

As you can see, a lot can be said in a few words and key words can be insinuated into the text seamlessly and with dramatic results.

Tip: Be concise. Don't give away your entire plot. Make sure your text is easy to follow. Don't include subplots or more than a couple of characters. Dangle a carrot and leave them wanting MORE.

1. **Strong Denouement:** Icing on the cake. Some authors use cliffhangers, hint at future danger or end their book descriptions with a question to make readers wonder what the main character will do next.

2. **In Closing:** Write a blurb about yourself or a personal note to the reader.

Marketing Magic: It's in the details

Creating superior marketing materials isn't easy. It takes effort, imagination and some skill.

Because of the millions of books available these days at the click of a mouse, it isn't enough to be an accomplished writer. You need to master some basic marketing skills to stay afloat. Think of your book description as ad copy ... to make it effective, you'll need to learn how to entice, hook and grab potential customer's interest by appealing to their needs or desires.

Of course it may be easier to pitch a Jaguar XKE or a Pepsi-Cola than a Romance novel but the underlying concepts are the same. If your text is as elegant, exclusive and appealing as a Jag or as spicy, refreshing and young as a Pepsi, you will increase your book sales.

The outline:

3. **Headline**: This should be something memorable and not necessarily a replica of your book title.

4. **Hook line or tag line:** An attention-grabbing sentence (or two) summarizing your plot that also entices a reader into your story.

Tip: Your "hook line" is the first pitch to a potential book buyer. The text should include mention of your main character and what he or she is trying to accomplish or overcome.
Examples:
(From Randy Ingermanson at advanced**fiction**writing)

Harry Potter and the Sorcerer's Stone: A boy wizard begins training and must battle for his life with the Dark Lord who murdered his parents.

The Hunger Games: A fight to the death – on live TV.

The Lord of the Rings: A hobbit learns that his magic ring is the key to saving Middle Earth from the Dark Lord.

The Time Traveler's Wife: A young girl grows up in the company of a strange time-traveling visitor who appears and disappears at random.

Pride and Prejudice: A young English woman from a peculiar family is pursued by an arrogant and wealthy young man.

Effective hook lines can also be in the form of questions, quotes or anecdotes. Experiment with different approaches and tones until you pinpoint 1) what works best for you combined with 2) the style of book you are writing.

A brief accolade: One sentence of endorsement or praise – preferably from a known or respected source like a best-selling or award-winning author of similar books; a local newspaper or magazine critic; a college professor; an expert in the field; etc.

5. **Book Description:** Keep it concise, in third person and active voice using 300 to 350 words or less.

GREAT TOOL: Free e-book on writing better Amazon descriptions, CLICK HERE.

Chapter 4: Sell more Kindle Books using proper keywords

By now you should understand the value and power of keywords. When used appropriately, they will help you outsell the competition every time. Like everything else, becoming adept at keyword identification is a process and one that will take time and effort on your part. But this is a necessary skill-set for any author promoting his or her own work. And it couldn't be simpler:

1. Discover Applicable Keywords
2. Use Keywords To Your Utmost Benefit

Google and Amazon keyword search tools are the most popular and since these Internet giants drive the most traffic online, we recommend using both. Following is an overview on the how-to.:

Google and Amazon Keyword Research

A. ADWORD PLANNER

Google has recently changed their keyword research tool kit to make it more user friendly for online marketers. Even if you are not familiar with keyword searches, you can still use Google **Adword Planner** for basic research.

Here's how:

Go to http://www.*adwords.google.com* and either create an account or log in to your existing account. First, click on the

Tools and Analysis link at the top of the page and then click and choose **Keyword Planner**.

On the left of your screen you will see three choices for keyword searches; click on the top one: **"Search for keyword and ad group ideas."** You can now begin your keyword search. For example, I might want to write a book about marketing ebooks on Kindle, so the first keywords I might try are "ebook marketing."

Google Tools will offer a list of phrases using your keywords along with data on the number of corresponding monthly searches for each phrase. Google will even reveal how competitive each word or phrase is – including how many other people and websites are using the identical language for their product or services.

We recommend not picking those options with the most fellow contenders. It will be harder to rank high in Google search results with so much competition.

Simple Steps for Beginners

Pick words that could be in your book title or that will inform readers what your book is about. For our book, *Sell more Ebooks,* we would type in, "sell ebooks." Google's suggested terminology tells us how many times people are looking for those keywords every month.

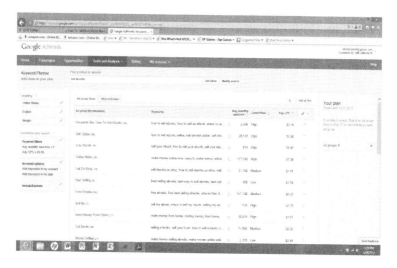

Tip: Pick Phrases that score at least 200 monthly searches yet have a low number of competitors.

Now pick one of the suggested essential phrases. For us, it would be the top one, "how to sell ebooks, how to sell an ebook, where to sell ebooks ..." Reading down the list, we see the term "sell ebooks" is a highly searched phrase so it's an attractive choice. At the same time, however, we see too many other people have already had the same idea, so we continue scanning the phrase list and noting other popular terms with less contenders.

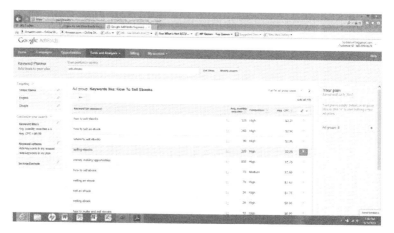

Tip: Pick four to seven phrases to use in your book title, description and/or interior content and jot them down so you can compare them to keywords on Amazon.

B. AMAZON RESEARCH TOOLS:

Now navigate to Amazon: http://www.amazon.com. On the left side of the search box, click on the small arrow to access a drop box.

NOTE: Make sure to click on Kindle Store before starting your inquiries. Once on Amazon's Kindle Store, type in the keywords you discovered on Google.

Continuing with our example, we would enter "sell ebooks." As you can see from the screen, before we finished typing, Amazon gave us their five top choices of the words or phrases people click on most.

Tip: The information provided from Amazon is your GO sign. If you use one or more of these terms in the title, description and/or tags of your ebook, it will start showing up on different Amazon search lists created by consumers looking for a product EXACTLY LIKE YOURS.

For example, if you enter: "sell more ebooks," you'd discover that our book, $ell more Ebook$ - how to increase sales and Amazon Rankings using Kindle Direct Publishing, is the first title listed.

Because we are listed with "Kindle Direct Publishing," and because we used those three words on our cover, our book will also appear under "ebook marketing KDP searches." We are #11 on that list.

And last but certainly not least, when potential customers search the phrase "Amazon rankings," our book is #8 on that list.

Note: Rankings listed here were current as of the publishing date of this book. Keep in mind that rankings change often on Amazon and our contemporary listing could be somewhat higher or lower. We offer the examples only to help you navigate the system.

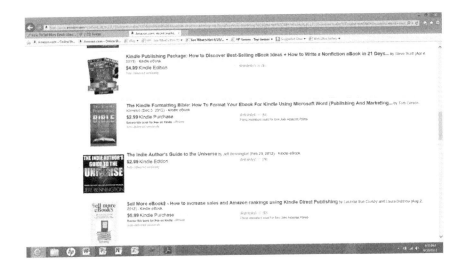

Tip: As a bonus, our carefully researched choice of book description and tags means that our title will show up on other ebook marketing lists as well. This is actually free publicity from

Amazon and boosts sales without us doing a dang-blasted thing. We will provide more in-depth information on book tags and descriptions later ... but basically you post the information when uploading your titles for publication at Kindle Direct Publishing.

One final piece of advice: If your keywords are recommended by Google **and** Amazon, you have hit the jackpot. When you use your terminology properly – placing your "catchphrases" in your book title, description and tags – more people looking for a product like yours will FIND YOU, leading to more sales.

C. OTHER RESEARCH TIPS:

When searching for impinging keywords, be careful to pick words and phrases that will point your targeted readers to your product. In other words, don't pick a word you think will get a lot of traffic but may not convert to any sales.

We published a book, _The Adventures of Baylard Bear – a story about being DIFFERENT_ – that is about a baby bear that is raised in a human orphanage and adopted by a human mom. The story illustrates the concept about being and feeling out of place in groups or settings outside the little bear's comfort zone.

When considering keywords, the first one that seemed logical was "adoption." But that word was going to be too general and could draw traffic from people seeking how-to information on the topic rather than someone looking for a child's chapter book. By using the phrase "adoption stories" instead, we tapered our focus to potential online browsers. Obviously, traffic will be less for "adoption stories," than for the stand alone, "adoption," phrase but our sales conversion rate will be higher.

Choose multiple niches: Your books will usually have more than one theme.

As we stated above, *The Adventures of Baylard Bear* can be used to discuss bullying, social situations or family life. So you can repeat the process for each one of these sub-categories to develop additional bankable keywords.

You can also type in words and phrases in a Google search to see how people are using popular terms to continue their high ranking on search pages. For example, if you type in "Amazon," you will see thousands of titles with that name. What marketers are doing is capitalizing on the high visibility of Amazon by juxtapositioning it and other high-ranking keywords in their titles.

Here's a for instance:

Go to Google and in the search box type in: amazon book marketing. You will notice several different titles, mostly books sold at Amazon, with an Amazon link. However, if you scroll to the bottom, there are two headings not linked to Amazon. That is because the authors of these sites know how to manipulate keywords to their advantage.

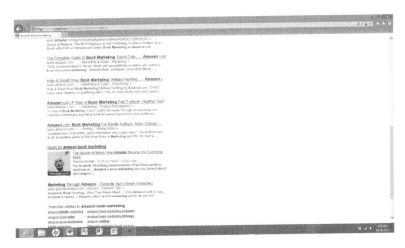

Eventually you will be using keywords with all your marketing efforts on social media forums including your blog. In the meantime, continue your research process until you have at least seven keywords or phrases that best fit your book.

Amazon allows 7 keywords for your Kindle titles: Here's how to use them for Ebook marketing

Now it's time to capitalize on your extensive keyword research, making a huge difference in the profitability of your book.

Amazon allows you to enter 7 keywords at the title level in your Kindle Direct Publishing account. Use all of them. Many authors don't bother listing any keywords at all and yet this is how people look for and find books. A lack of understanding about the important correlation between keywords and search results may be one reason for this oversight. We hope that YOU won't make this basic – and costly – mistake!

So let's take a closer look at this beneficial Amazon tool.
1. Customers, potential and otherwise, never see which keywords you selected. Yet, if you choose wisely, your book will magically appear when people type in certain phrases on the Amazon search box. This is a fantastic marketing tool. Here's how it works:

Let's say your novel is a romance. OK – but as we have discovered, the word "romance" will be too competitive:

A search in the Kindle Store for the word "Romance" will uncover a whopping 191,858 results! Holy guacamole! Unless your book is in the top 20 in the detail mode or the top 60 in the image mode, no one will see it. This is based on statistics demonstrating that most people stop browsing after the 3rd page.

If you narrow your search or make your keyword more specific, you'll have much better results. Our book, *Francesca of Lost Nation* is a romance novel with an old-fashioned story line. During our keyword investigation, we learned that the phrase, "old fashioned romance," had only 66 results. This means that *Francesca of Lost Nation* would be placed on the front page of the Amazon search when in image mode and third on the third page in detail mode. Our chances for sales are therefore much greater than if our title were buried somewhere in the 191,858 titles under "romance." (**Figures as of December 2013**).

Tip: This is why word and phrase research is essential. Notice, you need to find words that are searched enough to warrant potential sales, while not so competitive that you would be lost in the shuffle.

Keywords can be easily changed

Amazon allows you to change your Kindle Book keywords at any time. Ideally, you should check on their effectiveness 2-3 weeks after you list them. If you book has climbed into the top 20 in your sub-category, don't change a thing. If it's further down the list, give it an extra month or two to move up. If you do not see upward movement of your title, it's time to search for better phrases.

Tip: You can also try adding your keywords to your book title or book description. It's important to strike a balance here - don't change a title or sub-title too often but don't become complacent either. Note: Even the most successful keyword campaigns can have a shelf life. So, once you find something that works stick with it until it doesn't work and then change gears.

> 1.) What to keep out: Don't list your title, byline or book price. Amazon doesn't like typos, so edit carefully. (Some people purposely use typos on Google as a marketing trick – a topic for a different day.)

Tip: Amazon automatically uses your book titles, bylines and book prices to promote books on their site and on search boxes. Don't waste time repeating these tasks.

How to Get the Most from Your Keywords

When possible include phrases with your title, subtitle, descriptions and in the headlines, subheads and articles on your website. Using your main wordage in the name or description of your website should also be considered.

If you haven't released your book or built a website yet, incorporate these concepts before publishing. Authors using Print on Demand can revise their books easily and for little expense. If you have already printed 100 or more copies, don't spend more money. Make the changes on your digital files and on your website. Learn from your errors and move on to the next project.

On Amazon: When you upload your title at Createspace or Kindle Direct Publishing Select you will be given a section for your keywords and one for your book description. The keywords are not displayed publically but are used by Amazon, Google and the invisible web spiders to crawl through cyberspace and find people who are looking for matches to your phrases. You get only seven so pick wisely.

When it comes to your book description, use as many of the 4,000 characters as you can without repeating yourself. Sprinkle it with keywords but don't make it obvious. Write as though you were speaking to a friend.

On Website: When posting articles or information on your sites, filter keywords in the same manner as your book descriptions. Write conversationally. If you update your site at least once a week with fresh content and continue using your keywords, your site will automatically start climbing in rank.

If you have an author site that doesn't get updated often, you can keep your ranking high by having vivid descriptions, headlines and content. Only promote your book and site link now and then to generate traffic.

On Social Forums: Some authors will make use of Squidoo and article submission sites as well as guest posting on book or writing blogs. Make use of your keywords without being obvious – using your catch phrases four to five times throughout a 400 to 500 word article with a link or two in your signature box is enough promotion.

As you can see, finding and using keywords isn't simple but it is effective. Since the categories you select for your book placement will be equally as significant, let's take a look at that next.

Chapter 5: The Right Book Categories help you Sell Books

Amazon provides several categories which make it easier for an Indie author to become a Kindle Bestseller on these lists but for some inexplicable reason Amazon has made navigating category listings very complicated.

When publishing your book through the Kindle Direct Publishing platform, you will select two Kindle Bookstore categories for your title. However, finding the proper categories to make your book more visible for consumers is tricky. For instance, the Print categories are different than the Digital categories for your book. In addition, finding your subcategories is confusing in the KDP setup. Yet it is important to get your title in the proper group for better sales and it will require extra effort on your part.

Time consuming but beneficial in the long run: look for book titles in similar categories to yours and making note of the listing. While researching other titles you should also consider the following:

Number of books per category – you want a list with a low competition ratio.

Also familiarize yourself with the different category lists. This is where your keyword savvy will prove most helpful.

For example, for our title, *Francesca of Lost Nation*, an award-winning novel, with a family theme (an adventure story with a grandmother and her granddaughter as main characters), we have listed it in the following categories:

Kindle Store > Kindle eBooks > Literature & Fiction > Genre Fiction > Family Life

As of October 2013, it isn't ranked very high on the overall sales list but in the smaller category groups, we are in the "top 100" so our sales continue to stay steady. One of our keywords is "old-fashioned romance," which has only 89 books listed and ours is currently ranked 51. But when we run promotions, we move it into the top 10 where people see it more often and our sales increase. Imagine if you can get your book in the top 10 or 15 on at least 7 lists – the amount of keywords allotted for each title in KDP.

Our other book, *Sell more Ebooks – How to increase sales and Amazon rankings using Kindle Direct Publishing*, is ranked number 1 when people search for keyword phrase, "Sell more Ebooks." So sales for this book are quite high even though our overall ranking isn't that high.

That is your goal, rank high, do it often and capitalize on high placing keywords in low competition categories.
Tip: Keep in mind that you can change your category settings at any time so nothing is set in stone. Also, if you don't want to deal with the frustration, simply choose the categories for your listings and send Amazon a note through their contact form on your KDP account and ask them to do the work for you.

Choosing categories: How to pick the correct two for your book
    a.   The more sub categories available for your genre the better.

If you have written fiction, you will be competing with 789,050 other titles in that genre as of October 2013. Nonfiction writers will battle against 46,639 as of October 2013. You'd have to sell a tremendous amount of books to appear in the top 100 in these two categories.

However, if you can get more specific, you can multiply your potential visibility. Say you have written a Science Fiction novel and it could fit in the post-Apocalyptic or Hard Science Fiction themes, list your book as follows:

Kindle Store > *Kindle eBooks* > *Science Fiction &
Fantasy* > *Science Fiction* > **Post-Apocalyptic**

Kindle Store > *Kindle eBooks* > *Science Fiction &
Fantasy* > *Science Fiction* > **Hard Science Fiction**

When you drill deep into categories like this, your book
actually gets a boost in sales because your title will list
at all the top-level categories above the one you have
chosen and in addition, if you start making good sales,
you will begin to appear on a number of "top 100" top
lists, thereby driving more purchases for your book.

b. **Learn from Amazon.**
   Amazon offers an in-depth process on how to best
   navigate the KDP Select process for authors publishing
   digitally on Kindle and even details the instructions for
   choosing categories for your titles.

   Amazon recommends the following criteria for
   discovering the best browser categories:
   (http://bit.ly/1fIW9kn)

   • Pick accurately: In other words don't place your
     fiction romance under memoirs or your how-to
     books under history novels. You want to choose
     categories that best describe the genre.

Tip: Keep in mind if you have selected good keywords,
consumers seeking your topic will be directed to your title and if
you placed it under the proper category, people searching books
in your genre will also find you. This is why keywords and
categories are so important.

   • Be specific: Amazon suggests the following,
     *"Customers looking for very specific topics will
     more easily find your book, and your book will be
     displayed in more general categories as well (for
     example, a book in the "FICTION > Fantasy >*

50

> *Historical" category will also show up in searches for general fiction and general fantasy books). You should only select a "General" category if your book is actually a general book about a broad topic."*

Tip: This is where subcategories help. Remember you want the most exposure for your book. Since only Amazon knows their algorithm why not follow their advice?

- Don't duplicate efforts: Don't place your book titles in a category and duplicate the listing in a category's sub-category. You want your book to display in a variety of searches so be accurate and take advantage of listing in separate classifications.

Tip: When uploading your book to KDP Select, you will be offered a list of categories. Look for categories with subcategories and when possible pick subcategories that also have subcategories. If, however, what you want isn't listed, you can communicate with Amazon directly through their contact email on your KDP Select account and they will set it up for you.

Here's how:

Choose "Non-classified" on the book category list. Then either ask Amazon to list your book a certain way or provide them the list like the one above:

Kindle Store > *Kindle eBooks* > *Science Fiction & Fantasy* > *Science Fiction* > ***Post-Apocalyptic***

Kindle Store > *Kindle eBooks* > *Science Fiction & Fantasy* > *Science Fiction* > ***Hard Science Fiction***

How to use your keywords and categories together

Many authors either aren't familiar with or don't take advantage of another very important inside tip from Amazon which is how to make your keywords and categories work together in order to rank well in the various topic listings.

Amazon tells us that in order to list your titles in certain sub-categories, you'll need to add search keywords (remember the seven allotted when you upload your title to KDP Select) in addition to the categories you choose for your title. Amazon even gives you a list of categories and keyword requirements.

We list the categories here, and you can click/link to the keywords provided at Amazon:

Romance

Science Fiction & Fantasy

Children's

Teen & Young Adult

Mystery, Thriller, & Suspense

Comics & Graphic Novels

Literature & Fiction

Tip: Amazon continues to update its list. If you need further assistance because your categories are not listed or you are confused on how to list your book, just email Amazon: https://kdp.amazon.com/self-publishing/contact-us.

In the next section we'll discuss book descriptions and then we will wrap it up with how to put it all together through built-in Amazon tools.

Chapter 6: How to create book descriptions that convert into sales

Entice. Hook. Sell. That is what your book description needs to accomplish for you to increase your rate-of-purchase. If you can't grab the reader with a scintillating definition of your story ... if you can't convince the customer to actually fork out the price of your product ... you are losing sales.

Authors these days have to be marketing savvy. The book description is an art form once the purview of especially trained or gifted copywriters. Now it's up to the author. Most newby authors are convinced their book is SO fantastic, it'll sell on its own. Unless you are an established writer with a huge following, no one will know or care about what you created after Aunt Nellie and the rest of your kin buy your book Yes, a great cover and catchy title might draw some interest but most people buy books based on the characters and the story.

The Author Marketing Club has conducted a lengthy study on book descriptions and found that books with "robust," "colorful," and "engaging" accounts can sell up to 15 percent more books than those that don't.

- **Note:** AMC - The Author Marketing Club is a service of Digital Book Launch, a company owned by Internet entrepreneur and best-selling author Jim F. Kukral. It is a great site with free and paid promotional services for authors. We are premium members as well as affiliates and highly recommend these services.

Tips on writing great sales copy

Amazon allows you 4,000 characters. Use them all and craft them wisely.

1. Start with a headline – Make it active voice, use vivid language and provide the reader with a benefit.
2.

For example, the headline for the description of our book, _Sell more Ebooks – how to increase Sales and Amazon rankings using Kindle Direct Publishing_ is:

"Learn How to make Your Book a Kindle Bestseller"
Authors seeking to become bestsellers or wanting to learn how to sell more books will probably read beyond our headline to see if the book offers what they are looking for.
For our children's book, _The Adventures of Baylard Bear – a story about being DIFFERENT_, we used the following headline:
Being different can be a heavy burden at any age, but for a child?

Don't be afraid to use accolades in your description headline. If you have won an award or have a raving review from a known critic like Kirkus Reviews, use it. You can have a headline and a subhead too. For our multi-award-winning Romance Adventure novel, _Francesca of Lost Nation_:

A Must Read Novel – Romantic Suspense Kindle Book at its best

Winner of Four Literary Prizes / Author selected as one of "50 Authors You Should be Reading" by The Authors Show online media outlet

For our fourth title, _Water in the West: The Scary Truth about our most Precious Resource_, we have this description headline:

Will we run out of water? What, if anything, can we do to conserve it?

We just released a children's book which will be part of a series. Out title is <u>"Why is Pookie Stinky?</u> While some people might come across it by accident, no one would find it with search words unless seeking books with the name "Pookie" or the word "stinky." So we added the subhead: For Ages 4 to 7 Years Old (Book One: "Silly" Puppy Series).

When people search for ages 4 to 7 on Amazon, of 198 books, ours is listed at #1:

3. Description Content –

- Grab your reader's attention with a hook. Draw them in with a one to three sentences.
- Don't give away your plot
- Avoid subplots
- Introduce your main character(s) or villain
- Write in third person and active tense
- Target your audience – in other words don't sugar coat your content as a family friendly read if it isn't appropriate for children or if some adults would find your book offensive. You don't want to target Christian readers with Erotica – or maybe you do, so write your descriptions accordingly.
- End with a punch! – Leave 'em wanting more.

Here's an example of a good book description from the New York Times Bestseller, *Gone Girl: A Novel* by Gillian Flynn.

Description:
Headline: Marriage can be a real killer.
Content: *On a warm summer morning in North Carthage, Missouri, it is Nick and Amy Dunne's fifth wedding anniversary. Presents are being wrapped and reservations are being made when Nick's clever and beautiful wife disappears from their rented McMansion on the Mississippi River.*

Husband-of-the-Year Nick isn't doing himself any favors with cringe-worthy daydreams about the slope and shape of his wife's head, but passages from Amy's diary reveal the alpha-girl perfectionist could have put anyone dangerously on edge. Under mounting pressure from the police and the media—as well as Amy's fiercely doting parents—the town golden boy parades an endless series of lies, deceits, and inappropriate behavior. Nick is oddly evasive, and he's definitely bitter—but is he really a killer?

As the cops close in, every couple in town is soon wondering how well they know the one that they love. With his twin sister, Margo, at his side, Nick stands by his innocence. Trouble is, if Nick didn't do it, where is that beautiful wife? And what was in that silvery gift box hidden in the back of her bedroom closet? –
as posted on <u>Amazon</u>.

The description introduces the main characters, gives you an idea what the plot is about without giving away too much, targets an audience and makes you want to read more by dangling the answer to the mystery.

- Call to action – Don't forget to tell the reader to "Buy Now," or "Scroll to the top and Purchase."

- Other text to include – While not necessary you can also add an endorsement, brief author bio or call to action such as "Visit my website to learn more about me or my work." (Linking to Author Central is always a good idea)

3. **Bringing it altogether:** Advanced Marketing tips

Now you will see how your keywords, categories and book description all tie in together to help you market your books and make more sales.

a.   From Amazon itself:

To increase your book's discoverability on Amazon, you need descriptions and keywords that accurately portray your book's content and use the words customers will use when they search. Along with factors like sales history and Amazon Best Sellers Rank, relevant keywords can boost your placement in search results on Amazon.com. (http://bit.ly/16tz7Ex)

Tip: If you have a non-fiction book such as a How-To topic, it is advisable to filter your seven keywords into your book description without making it obvious. Always write conversationally and use proper grammar.

For fiction, filter only one to two words into your description. For example you can include a sentence like this, "In this light romantic comedy the main characters run off with a quirky preacher ...) It tells the reader your genre and uses keywords you probably listed.

Note: You can change your descriptions and keywords as often as you like on KDP Select so feel free to experiment until you find something that works. Then stick with it as long as you are making sales.

Making it all stand out

Now that your copy is ready, you want to make it stand out. Amazon allows html coding that will help your book descriptions stand out. For instance your Book Description headlines can be in big bold lettering and you're allowed subheads and bullets to make your content eye-popping.

A master at this is bestselling author and book marketing expert, Tom Corson-Knowles. He has written many books on the topic and includes the coding you will need at his blog: TCK Publishing.

Tom will show you how to customize your book description using HTML and you will be able to have fancy orange headlines with italics, bold font and underlines.

In addition, The Author Marketing Club, offers tools for this same purpose but you have to sign up to be a premium member (currently $105 a year or $29.95 per month). We are affiliates and highly recommend the service. Click here for details: Author Marketing Club.

In the next section, we will show you how to market your book with all the Amazon built-in promotion tools.

Chapter 7: Take advantage of Amazon – your best book publicity tool

Amazon is the world's largest online retail book store. If you list a book and leave it there, it may never sell more than a few copies but if you take the time to understand the built-in publicity tools Amazon offers, you could become a bestseller even if you never published a book before.

INDY authors should take advantage of Amazon's automated system which works to advertise all its books whether self-published or not. Unfortunately many authors either don't know about these promotional layers or don't know how to use them. In fact you can actually rank in the top 100 on several high-profile lists without selling one book because landing on one of these lists could generate sales.

Following is an overview of the various lists. In the next section, we will look at marketing methods that can help you get onto these lists.

Category Bestseller
Remember the narrower your target audience the better so list your book in tightly aimed sub-categories.

Keep in mind that category and subcategory best seller lists were created by Amazon to highlight an item's rank in those listings. Think of it as a new old-fashioned "come on." Coincidentally, it also makes it easier for customers to find specific items. While ranking high doesn't necessarily guarantee sales, being a bestseller = visibility = sales.

Tip: According to Amazon, this is how they operate their category rankings.

"As with the main Amazon Best Sellers list, category rankings are based on Amazon.com sales and are updated hourly.

- *For the Kindle Store, Amazon Best Seller lists are divided into Top 100 Paid and Top 100 Free. Both lists are updated hourly.*
- *For competitive reasons, Amazon.com generally does not publish this information to the public."*

Top Rated List

The more book reviews in general and the more positive reviews specifically, the better chance of landing in the Top 100. Amazon's automated system finds and tallies the number of reviews each book has earned and also calculates the star ratings. Ergo, the more good reviews your book has the higher it will rank on the Top Rated list.

- You want good book reviews. While you have no control on what people say about your book, you do have some say on obtaining book reviews.

  a. Pitch your book to people who may enjoy your genre
  b. Offer a book giveaway at reader blogs
  c. Use author friendly sites such as Smashwords, Goodreads and World Literary Café to request book reviews. Don't forget to use Amazon forums. Your social media sites like Facebook, Linkedin and Twitter can be helpful too.
  d. Include a book review request inside all your books

Top Rated – for Kindle books only

Based entirely on customer reviews, this list takes into account an item's total number of reviews and compares it against other items within a category or subcategory. The more 4 or 5 star ratings your book gets, the better overall average for you. Newer reviews outrank older ones.

Customer favorites Top 100 of the year
The more annual sales you make the higher you will rank.

Best books of the month
Amazon editors choose these but forget about discovering their criteria – it's a well-kept trade secret. We know because we've tried to find out!.

Bestsellers in Books
Top 100 bestselling books sold by every author in every category combined, updated hourly.

Best Books of the Year
Amazon editors select these titles. While their whys and hows are also closely guarded, it seems logical that books with great reviews, sales and publicity tend to make the list.

Amazon has many other lists. Each is designed to highlight books and make more sales. So if you have a quality product, use keywords, categories, descriptions and Amazon tools wisely, it will help you generate more visibility and higher profits.

Amazon also offers a variety of book promotion programs. Unfortunately, Amazon hasn't integrated its different divisions into one section, so for every program at Amazon, you will need to log in separately for each platform and fill out your information.

Here's an overview of Amazon programs that also help promote your books:

    a.   **Audio** – ACX is a program offered through Amazon that allows you to produce a digital audiobook version of your book which is integrated with the new Whispersync for Voice on Kindle. The product is a professionally-narrated work.

b. **Look Inside the Book** – this allows customers to skim a portion of your book before deciding on the purchase. Take advantage of this feature by offering enticing text at the start of your work – this means going against the grain of traditional publishing that sets credits, dedications, copyright and table of contents at the front of a book.

c. **Author Central** – This section is like a mini-blog at Amazon. Take advantage of this section with good content, images, interesting tidbits about you and your books. You can also add social media links and book appearance information here.

d. **Amazon Advantage** – This forum works best for small press publishers or book vendors needing distribution and warehousing at reasonable rates.

e. **KDP Select** – This is Amazon's Digital Book Platform and probably the most beneficial for authors. With KDP Select, you can use your book titles, descriptions, categories and keywords to make your book more visible. KDP Select also offers authors free book promotion days and enrollment in the Kindle Lending Library – two programs that give writers visibility and profits.

Amazon has also added three new programs: Kindle Matchbook, Kindle Countdown Deal and Kindle Prime Membership. We are going to take a closer look at how to use KDP Select and the new 2014 programs in the next section.

Part II

Marketing, Marketing, Marketing:

Free Days, Book Reviews, Social Media and other publicity ideas

Chapter 8: How to Navigate KDP Select – Use your Free Days Strategically

With the changing landscape of book marketing and promotion, who has time to write? Marketing does take up a lot of time but it's a necessity for book sales. Even if you publish through a traditional agency, you will have to promote your product, so it is better to understand the process even if you hire someone else to do it.

Keep in mind Amazon reported more than 121 million active customers in 2009. Since it stopped reporting these figures, no one knows how this number compares today but the sales potential HUGE. Don't miss out on an amazing opportunity just because the process seems daunting.

Let's get started.

First steps

After you have written a quality book and have it professionally edited, follow the next steps and publish on Kindle Direct Publishing Select. You can either use Createspace or upload the book yourself at: https://kdp.amazon.com

a. Choose a good cover, title and seven solid keywords
b. Determine your 2 categories and narrow your choices to tight subcategories
c. Write a great book description
d. List your book on Kindle Direct Publishing Select

Amazon Kindle Direct Publishing

The year 2011 became self-publisher friendly when Amazon introduced KDP Select allowing authors to offer books for free. Writers are offered five days, which can be used in a block or in intervals, within a 90-day window – with exclusivity for that term required by Amazon.

In addition, book titles enrolled in the program are offered in the Kindle Owner's Lending Library through which Amazon Prime customers are able to borrow one title per month.

At firs, authors were hesitant to give Amazon full control of their product for 3 months. But the complaints soon disappeared in the whirlwind of success stories. Overnight, obscure titles were hitting bestseller lists all over the book retailer's site. Unknown authors were getting their books into reader's hands and some self-publishers went into profit mode nearly overnight after years of struggling.

A big reason for this success was the fact that free downloads were counted as a full paid sale in the popularity lists. A free-day run with 1,000 downloads could boost a title into a top 100 bestseller list and someone with 10,000 downloads would jump to the top 10 in a category. This resulted in many authors riding the wave of popularity for a few weeks even after their book was no longer free. Many authors became wealthy, particularly those that jumped at the opportunity and published several books during the ride.

In addition, Amazon used to list the top 100 paid books side by side with the top 100 Free books – placing many INDY authors next to a New York Times bestseller.

All good things end.

Amazon changed the rules in March 2012. KDP Select is no longer a sure thing.

The top 100 Free books list is hidden behind a tab and no longer runs side by side with the paid list. Freebies are now worth one-tenth of a paid sale on the Popularity Lists – this means 1,000 free downloads would be equivalent to 100 sales and possibly not a large bump in your overall standings.

So why bother?

FREE Days can still generate book sales

Although the nuts and bolts have been rearranged, FREE days are still a key marketing tool for INDY writers.

For most writers and authors, traditional publishing wasn't working. The big-name book sellers were operating as if the Internet didn't exist and Amazon jumped at the opportunity. Their program became so successful they had no choice but to change the rules in order to keep track.

All of us need to do the same. After all WE helped fuel the fire and made the popularity of ebooks what it is today. So here's to moving forward!!

Adjusting to change: (Change? Did someone say CHANGE??!!)

- **Have Free Promotions less frequently:** When we first started using KDP Select, we ran free days every six weeks and it helped us with steady sales but as the free day changes were put into place it became evident that we needed to stagger our FREEBIES.

  Many of the free-day listing websites or paid-free-day promotion advertising companies have also started charging for their services to recoup money lost from other Amazon administration and operating changes that affect affiliates. This means you will have to budget more for advertising and that listing less frequently could be financially beneficial.

Tip: Experiment with new categories and keywords with each promotion unless you are rackig up sales. And don't stop marketing your book in other ways – guest blog posts, social media, or paid advertising – during the periods between FREEBIE promos.

Longer Promotions: We use to advise breaking up the five free days when we were investing in frequent KDP

Select promotions. But these days, it seems smarter to promote 3 to 5 days in a row since a book needs more downloads to move up in the rankings.

Tip: Run your promotions when you can advertise on as many free and paid forums as possible to create high volume on all of your promo dates. This will require notifying the sites in advance and having the money to pay up front for some services.

- **Schedule promotions last days of the month:** We don't know why, but this time frame seems to be when most downloads occur. In addition, Amazon Prime Members tend to make their library borrows the first few days of every month. Between your end-of-the-month downloads and the start of new month borrows, your book has the greatest potential of landing on one of the Amazon lists.

Tip: Experimentation is the order of the day. If you find something that works, do it again. When it stops working change it up. Keep in mind if others are doing the same, you will have competition listing your book at all the desirable promotion sites so plan ahead and spend wisely.

Setup and Advertising Free Days:

Here's a quick overview,
1. Choose effective keywords
2. Pick two categories
3. Write a spot-on book description
4. Select your promotion dates for listing your book free
5. Announce your free days 14 to 30 days ahead at all relevant promotion sites
6. Be ready for promo days

(for step-by-step instructions, purchase our book *Sell more Ebooks – how to increase sales and Amazon rankings using Kindle Direct Publishing* or go to Amazon.)

Your action Plan:

There are several sites that will post your KDP Promotions for FREE. Others require payment for a **guaranteed** placing, including our site, <u>Kindle Book Promos</u>. This is due to Amazon changes in how it promotes free books and how it pays its affiliates – people like us that promote Amazon books.

Are you ready to promote? Make sure your book is properly listed, formatted, titled and has an interesting and appropriate cover. Be prepared to list your book at numerous sites on the day of promotions, be willing to respond to emails and blog requests and follow up your free days with additional marketing.

1. **Pick your titles and dates**: It's easier to run one book promotion at a time but if you can organize and handle more than one go for it. Determine how many days you will use of the five available – we recommend 3 to 5 to build momentum and to accumulate as many downloads as possible. Then wait 60 to 90 days or longer before running the next promotion. EXCEPTIONS ... if you see momentum or have a budget for more promotion, you might try 30 to 45 days. Also keep in mind you a maximum of 5 days total within a 90 day window – so if you use all 5 days in your initial promotion, you will have to wait for your next 90 day slot.

Tip: Select the dates carefully with an eye on upcoming noted "buying holidays" like the biggest shopping day of the year – "Black Friday," – or the day after Christmas and New Year's when a lot of new Kindle owners will be looking for books to load onto their new toys.

2. **Advertise Free Days:** The more sites and forums that hear about your book, the more successful your campaign. Get the news out to every social site you frequent and post to every network open to book promotions.

Tip: We suggest you have a separate email account attached to your KDP promos. Many of the sites listed below require you to register for newsletters or notifications and your email box will overflow! You can always opt-out of any subscriptions once you end your promotions. Be sure to read and comply with all site guidelines. And beware ... listings like these can change or disappear without notice.

These three sites offer a list of Free Promotion Listings and submission tools for FREE:

FREE Kindle Book Submission Tool

Over 120 sites to promote your FREE DAYS

Great Author Tools – lots of helpful links

BONUS: Get Featured: INDY SPOTLIGHT at www.rickiwilson.com

Here are some of the top sites we use to promote our KDP-Select Free Days:

http://bit.ly/192zUE

http://bookpraiser.com/submit-book/

http://bit.ly/1pFN5Pj

http://www.fkbooksandtips.com/for-authors/regular-book-posting/

http://www.thekindlebookreview.net/

http://www.pixelofink.com/sfkb/

http://digitalbooktoday.com/12-top-100-submit-your-free-book-to-be-included-on-this-list/

http://worldliterarycafe.com/

http://kindlenationdaily.com/

http://freebooksy.com/

Here are sites we recommend for paid advertising of your FREE DAYS:
(Remember there are no guarantees for book sales.)

https://kindlebookpromos.luckycinda.com – (Our site offers very reasonable prices)

https://www.bookbub.com/partners/pricing - (Your book has to be accepted first)

http://www.booktweetingservice.com/ - (A bit pricey but good service with large audience)

http://www.booksends.com/advertise.php - (Fairly new site but run by a savvy author/marketer)

http://www.bookgorilla.com/advertise - (Fairly new site)

http://digitalbooktoday.com/ - (Great site, good promotion opportunities and run by a book-savvy author and all-around great guy)

http://www.thekindlebookreview.net/ - (Operated by a best-selling author and his team who are very helpful to authors.)

http://www.kboards.com/index.php/topic,11400.0.html – (Slots fill up fast so make sure to coordinate your promo days accordingly.)

Use Twitter and Facebook on the Day of your Promotions:

Note: Be careful not to spam – spread your tweets throughout the promotion dates. Don't blast every 10 minutes to each site. You should post to Facebook sites only once per day unless you have permission by the site administrator to do otherwise. And since Facebook has very strict rules about free advertising, don't get kicked off.

Use the following hashtags on Twitter to promote your free days:

#kindle
#kindlefire
#ebooks
#FREE
#mustread
#goodreads
#greatreads
#freeebooks
#Kindlefreebooks
#AmazonPrime
#Kindledeals
#kindledeals

Example: Winner of 5 literary awards, #FREE today on #kindle: (your link here)

You can also hashtag genre references, like #romance, #mystery, #nonfiction – whatever applies to your title. Or hashtag your audience, for example if your book has an educational target: #teachers, #education or #learningtools.

Also let these Twitter sites know about your free books and ask for a retweet or mention. For example if you wanted us to retweet your free book day, you would contact us either @freebookpromos or @penabook.

This is how:

@freebookpromos Pls RT: #FREE today (your title or genre) on #kindle: (your link)
(Remember you only have 140 characters total – so keep it short).

Here are other sites: (There are many so don't limit your promotion to these – you can search for more on Twitter using the search box or add to your list as you come across sites in books or other blogs you use):

@FreeKindleStuff
@FreeReadFeed
@free_kindle
@Freebookdeal
@freebookpromos
@freebooksy
@KindleBookBlast
@KindleDaily
@Kindlbookreview
@digitalBKtoday
@KindleFreeBooks
@kindle_mojo
@Kindlefreebies
@kindlenews
@freebookpromos
@penabook
@Kindlestuff
@KindleEbooksUK
@KindleBookKing
@4FreeKindleBook
@freebookclub1
@ibdbookoftheday
@Booksontheknob
@bookbub
@kindle_free
@freeebooksdaily
@kindlefreebooks

@zilchebooks
@freedailybooks
@free2kindle
@freereadfeed
@pixelofink
@digitalinktoday
@fkbt
@kindlestuff
@free_kindle_fic
@Bookyrnextread
@CheapKindleDly
@DigitalBkToday
@kindlenews
@ebook
@freeebookdeal
@free
@free_kindle
@freebookdude
@4FreeKindleBook
@FreeKindleStuff
@IndAuthorSucess
@IndieKindle
@kindleebooks
@KindleBookKing
@KindleFreeBook
@KindleUpdates
@Kindle_promo
@KindleDaily
@WLCPromotions

Facebook sites that allow free book day postings:

https://www.facebook.com/ebookpromos

https://www.facebook.com/AontheC

https://www.facebook.com/iauthor?sk=wall

https://www.facebook.com/IndieKindleWLC

https://www.facebook.com/kindle

https://www.facebook.com/indiebookslist

https://www.facebook.com/ebooksfreefreefree

https://www.facebook.com/mobileread

https://www.facebook.com/freebooktoday

https://www.facebook.com/TheKindleBookReview

https://www.facebook.com/Freebooksy - **(Has a list of other Free Book Listing Sites)**

https://www.facebook.com/FreeBookClub.org

https://www.facebook.com/OneHundredFreeBooks

https://www.facebook.com/DigitalBookToday

https://www.facebook.com/freeebooksdotnet

https://www.facebook.com/IAmAReader

https://www.facebook.com/bookclubbooks

https://www.facebook.com/BookClubGirl

https://www.facebook.com/thereadingroomonline

https://www.facebook.com/BookRiot

https://www.facebook.com/pages/Kindle-Bestseller-Secrets/195560307296759

https://www.facebook.com/groups/270558336379692/

https://www.facebook.com/groups/FreeTodayOnAmazon/

https://www.facebook.com/authormarketingclub

https://www.facebook.com/BookGoodies

https://www.facebook.com/galleycat/app_4949752878

https://www.facebook.com/IndieBookLounge

https://www.facebook.com/IndieKindleWLC

http://www.facebook.com/weloveebooks

http://www.facebook.com/StoryFinds

http://www.facebook.com/pages/UK-Kindle-Book-Lovers/175617412524192

Post on these sites 24 hours in advance or on the day of your promotion:

http://snickslist.com/books/place-ad/

http://www.freebookclub.org/kindle-books/book-submissions/

http://addictedtoebooks.com/free

http://www.daily-free-ebooks.com/suggest-free-ebook

http://www.ereaderiq.com/contact/

New FREE DAY Strategies 2014 and 2015

KDP –Select: Amazon is always changing things around, usually with little fanfare … so be alert. For instance, when submitting your titles to KDP-Select, there is now a section that allows you to target an age group! Coyly, it is marked "optional" – USE IT. To our knowledge, Amazon has never publicized this feature but it can get your product seen in more categories and exposed to new readers.

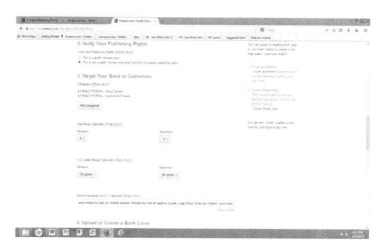

Just click on the arrows and select from the lists provided: Age range and school grade.

Additionally, there is a little known trick regarding keywords. While Amazon allows you only seven keywords, here's a way to get a few more in.

Try to select two to three keyword/phrases for your first six keywords. For example, if you have written a romance adventure novel, use the full phrase, "romance adventure novel" as your first keyword. Your second keyword should come from the list of researched phrases you found on Amazon and Google Ad Tools. So you might have something like, "romance kindle books" or "romance books for kindle 2014." Each phrase is separated by a comma and each phrase is considered one keyword. But when consumers are searching, any combination of words or phrases will take readers to a list of books referenced by these keywords. If you get yours in the right sequence and can sell enough to be in the top 20, you will start making even more sales.

Here's an example of how you would list the keywords discussed above:

Romance kindle books, romance books for kindle 2014, romance adventure novel (then add three more stand-alone keywords or two- to three-word phrases: old-fashioned love, erotic novels, romantic adventure.

Tip: On your seventh keyword make it as long as possible but it should still make sense. Some authors just add 8 to 10 words with no commas but we think it should be a logical phrase that a reader may be searching for – the latter seems to have a higher sales conversion rate, at least for us. Experiment with what works for you.

Example: For our first marketing book, Sell more Ebooks – how to increase sales and Amazon rankings using Kindle Direct Publishing, we targeted first time authors who know nothing

78

about digital publishing or how to get started on Kindle sales. Since our book can fall into the Kindle categories of Direct Sales, Authorship, Online Marketing, How to Sell more Ebooks and Reference – we might use the following phrase as our last keyword:

Marketing guide for authors learning online marketing, how to sell more ebooks and make direct sales – see how many keywords were used but in a comprehensive phrase. Readers searching terms like "marketing guide," "sell more ebooks," or "online marketing," will probably see our book.

Currently, anyone that types in "sell more ebooks" into Amazon's search engine in the Kindle Books section, will get a list of over 400 books. Ours is #1 on that list.

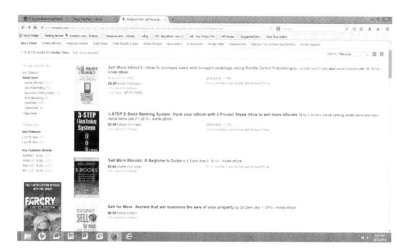

PROMO TOOLS:

Take advantage of all the tools available to authors in today's market. For example, Amazon now encourages writers to use special codes for descriptions under the book titles – the ones you see with the big Orange Headlines – once a "well-kept" secret. The Author Marketing Club, operated by Jim Kukral, offers a user friendly description-building tool for Amazon to its paid membership. TCK Publishing, operated by Tom Corson-Knowles, another book marketing expert, offers Do-it-Yourself authors the necessary codes at his website.

These book descriptions, if created properly, will boost your book rankings.

Author Page:
Amazon allows you to post an Author's Page which is similar to a blog. You can include detailed information about yourself and post pictures and videos along with links to your website and blogs. This is a great opportunity for you to connect with your readers.
Too many authors still don't advantage of this section. This is another free forum where your content, keywords and images can help you sell your books. Readers like to place a face and learn about an author's background. (Remember, selling is all about building a bridge between writer and reader.) How many times have you enjoyed a book and wanted to let the writer know. We appreciate the frustration you felt if you could not find a contact or even a blog. This is a great way to turn your audience off.

FACEBOOK: Along with your free site and paid listings as described earlier, you should consider some Facebook strategies, only available since early this year. You now have the option to promote posts from either your personal profiles or your fan pages. Just click "promote" under your post and follow the directions which will allow you to choose your target demographics. You can also choose your budget!

NOTE: We will examine Facebook in greater detail in Chapter 11.

GOODREADS: This forum offers scheduled giveaways for its readers and can attract up to 725 entrants. Although giving your product away may seem counterintuitive, who doesn't love to win a contest or an unexpected freebie? We wish to emphasize that self-promotion alone won't get the job done and too much can actually harm your outreach efforts. Forums are monitored and each has its own set of rules. Be sure to familiarize yourself with the ins and outs of each platform BEFORE using it. Now, if you're already an active member, don't forget to use Goodreads as an additional place to pitch your free books.

Note: We will also expand on the use of Goodreads in Chapter 11.

BLOG TOURS: If you have the budget, you should also schedule a blog tour to coincide with your free book promotions. Some tours will feature you and your book via personal interview post or book review. Each blog has its own set of rules and, once you and your book are accepted, you will be notified regarding what is needed and wanted for your tour. Again, there are no guarantees of downloads or sales of your titles, as audience participation, number of visitors to the site, the type of book you are promoting and other variables affect participation.

Here is a list of book tour sites we have used in the past with some success:

Expresso Book Tours – Has a large following, including nearly 3,000 members on Goodreads. Tours usually include 15 blog stops. Prices are reasonable.

Enchanted Book Promotions – Offers several tour options at affordable prices.

Bewitching Book Tours – A good place for Romance books.

Goddess Fish Promotions – Book in advance as this is a popular site with several opportunities to promote your titles.

Orangeberry Book Tours – Has been in the business over 10 years and excels in site management.

Reading Addiction Virtual Book Tours – Very affordable prices for authors.

Sage Book Tours – Author owned and operated. One of our faves!

IMAGES: Visual advertising is nothing new; online marketers have been using the power of video for years. Of course, the ease of image sharing with free and new software online has tripled the use of photographs in promotions.

Twitter has recently added the capability of paid advertising so posting images in ads is now encouraged. In addition, Twitter has updated its profile template pages, allowing authors to post image headers similar to Fan Pages on Facebook.

Note: We will take a closer look at Twitter promotions in Chapter 10.

The latest online sensation is a forum called Pinterest, similar to Goodreads and Facebook except it is visually driven. Like most social sites, you input your profile details, build conversation boards and share information. Instead of verbal discussions, photos and videos are the norm. If you haven't used Pinterest, it's worth a try.

Kimberley Grabas of Your Writer Platform has an in-depth blog on how to use Pinterest: *34 Strategic Ways You Can Use Pinterest to Market Your Book and Your Author Brand.*

There's also a good post on using Pinterest at **The Book Designer** (an overall fantastic blog for writers).

ADDING INCENTIVES: One of the quickest ways to get more traffic is to offer something to entice consumers to your links. Who doesn't love free stuff even when it's not expensive? You can give away a $25 Amazon gift card, autographed books by you and other authors, a free ad on your website, a $10 Starbuck's card or any slew of other prizes you cleverly conjure up.

We suggest running an Amazon Gift Card Giveaway along with your Free Day Book Promotion. This will allow you to get additional advertising for your book because you can link your Amazon Gift Card Giveaway to several sites not necessarily targeted to readers only. This new audience will download your book for a shot at the Amazon Gift Card.

Here's how it works:

Rafflecopter: This is an easy tool to use. Automated features include email capture, contest template, scheduling and picking winners at random.

We use this application for all our giveaways. Annually on our site Kindle Book Promos, we offer a Black Friday Special and Christmas Drawing with Kindle products and ebooks as prizes. Rafflecopter allows us to set up the template with unique contest entry terms.

As you can imagine, a set-up like this can drive a lot of traffic to your site. We usually require either a Retweet of our event, a Facebook Fanpage Like or a blog comment on our site. This activity boosts our page rank on Google too.

You can use your giveaway to entice people to download your FREE book for 5 or 10 extra entries toward an Amazon Gift Card or gift of your choice.

Many book promotion sites, like ours, use these giveaways to feature sponsors. We charge a small fee (between $25 and $50) to link other authors' books as sponsors alongside the Giveaways. Each title gets a blurb and is seen by hundreds of people as they sign up. As of July 2014, we average 15,000 visitors a month. In addition, we promote our giveaways at major promotion listing sites. Last year our Christmas giveaway netted more than 25,000 entries.

Rafflecopter is free: http://www.rafflecopter.com/
We also recommend signing up with major giveaway listing sites:
List your Blog Giveaway – also offers to set everything up for you for a small fee starting at $4.99
Blog Giveaway Directory
Fiverr: We have used these gigs with great success –
Adds your giveaway to 10 top sites for $5
Will post up to 100 Links for $15

Other good marketing ideas:
- Best-selling Author Hugh Howie (Kindle book *Dust (Silo Saga)* is currently #1 under post-apocalyptic and #4 under Science Fiction. This is no accident but a payoff from creative marketing.

Hugh created a special USB thumb-drive featuring the silo Fallout Shelter Sign, to give away to supporters who would help promote the book by spreading word-of-mouth buzz. Each USB stick contains his books WOOL, SHIFT, and DUST in both .epub and .mobi, with downloading directions for reading devices. He also includes an intriguing 'secret file'. – as posted on Bestseller Labs – Read Entire Post Here

- Learn from others – find the successful and glean from their expertise

I am a huge fan of Tom Corson-Knowles. This is a young man that is currently earning more than 10K a month through Kindle Direct Publishing. In addition, he took his blog from zero to over 100,000 page views per month and he did it in less than a year. He has his own publishing company and has authored many books.

His advice to authors:
"The difference between people who make a serious income online and those who can't earn a dollar online is that the successful people treat it like a business. If you're an author, realize that marketing is 80 percent of the formula for success as an author. The other 20 percent is how well you write." See full interview at Kindle Book Promos

Also see the following:
Authors sharing how they sold books using social media
Creative Marketing Ideas from 10 Great Thought Readers

As you can see, book marketing is a full-time occupation. There's no way around that so the best way to make it work for you is to find the tools that work for your promotional needs. Find one or two things that work consistently and stick with them until they stop working. We understand if you tried to accomplish everything in this book on a daily basis you would be a bestselling author but probably wouldn't have time to enjoy it – lack of sleep isn't recommended.

Our advice is to automate as much as possible, outsource if you can afford to do so and be creative. The more unique your publicity methods, the more success you'll have and the more time you'll find to write.

Ok let's move on and take a look at Amazon's new 2014 and 2015 book marketing features.

Chapter 9: Kindle Matchbook, Kindle Countdown Promos and $.99 Kindle Deals

In November 2013 Amazon launched two new programs: Kindle Matchbook and Kindle Countdown Promos. While these programs haven't seemed to catch on or work as effectively as the Kindle Direct Publishing Free Days, authors should still take advantage of these tools. In all likelihood, Amazon will probably continue to modify these platforms or integrate them into other promotions in 2015 and 2016. We predict this based on Amazon's innovations of the past few years considering the rollouts of their Amazon prime memberships, Kindle Fires and now with their Music Prime deals.

Let's take a look at how Kindle Matchbook and Countdown Promos can help you, the author.

Kindle Matchbook

This Amazon option is for readers who buy your printed books. It makes them eligible to get your ebook of the same title for $2.99 or less - and sometimes even for free. For authors, it means you can now make two sales instead of one for each of your titles to the same customer.

Here's how it works:

You must have both a print and digital version of your book for sale on Amazon. Your ebook does not have to be enrolled exclusively with Amazon but you will need to enroll your ebook in the Kindle Matchbook Program. You control both the price of your ebook and the length of time you want to be in the program.

When you are enrolled in Matchbook, every time a customer buys one of your print books, Amazon lets that person buy your ebook at a discount. Another plus is that readers can get this deal for any print book purchased all the way back to when Amazon first opened its online bookstore in 1995. Also any customer who has been gifted a printed book can buy the discounted ebook of the same title.

Using Matchbook for marketing:
We suggest setting your enrolled Matchbook ebooks at a discount price of .99. Our reasoning: If someone already paid $15 to $20 for your hard copy, .99 is a bargain and it also gives you a Kindle sale which boosts your rankings. If you offer your ebook at too high a price, it isn't much of an incentive for the reader and if you offer it for free, Amazon doesn't count it as a Kindle sale.

For authors who have been looking to sell more paperbacks, this may be a way to start moving inventory. Take advantage of Kindle Matchbook as an extra marketing tool when promoting your books on your website, at speaking engagements or on personal book tours.

Here's a great video by Tom Corson-Knowles on how to use Matchbook and how to set it up for your titles: <u>How to Use Kindle Matchbook to Sell more Books.</u>

Kindle Countdown Deals

This tool allows authors to run limited-time discounts on their ebooks. Your countdown deal can last up to a week and is a focused kind of sale. By using this program, you can continue to earn your selected royalty rate during the promotion. For example, instead of the 35 cents per ebook when priced at 99 cents (due to Amazon's 35 percent royalty for titles priced under $2.99), each sale would be worth 70 cents when selling the ebook for 99 cents during the countdown deal.

Amazon is still experimenting with Countdown Deals and hasn't advertised it as well as its KDP – Select Free promotions. Several authors have tried Countdown Deals and haven't been too enthusiastic about the program but, like most marketing plans, if executed properly, this tool can help you get more sales.

Advantages:

- You set the dates and the discount price, which means you can plan your marketing efforts in advance. Like the Free Day promos, there are sites available to advertise your deals, including a couple that can lead to a large number of downloads.

- Amazon has its own dedicated website for readers to view, making your titles more visible.

- Kindle Countdown offers a staggering "price raise" feature that allows authors and publishers to set the discounted price starting as low as 99 cents, then rising to $1.99 and eventually back to full price as the days go on. Amazon even posts a countdown clock next to your title alerting customers how long they have left until the sale ends.

Criteria:
1) Your book has to be enrolled in KDP Select for at least 30 days before a Kindle Countdown Deal can be triggered.
2) You cannot run a KDP Select free promotion and a Kindle Countdown Deal in the same 90-day period.
3) The program is only open to US and UK markets.

Using Countdown for marketing:
Here are the links to help you get started:

Getting Started:
To learn more about Kindle Countdown setup and how it works, go to this site:
Marketing EasyStreet.
Videos on Youtube:
For US Market
For UK Market

Sites to list your Countdown Deals:

USA

Kindle Book Promos – offering free and paid listings for countdown deals.

ereadernewstoday.com – accepting books priced at 99c or lower. Your book will need to have at least 10 reviews with at least a 4 star average rating.

Pixel of Ink - accepts submissions for books priced at 99c or lower.

.efictionfinds.com - accepts submissions for books priced at $2.99 and under. You will need a minimum of 10 reviews, with a 4.0 average rating.

feedyourreader.com - listing books up to $3.99, except on Sundays.

bargainebookhunter.com offering guaranteed listings of 99c books for $10 each and a similar service for books priced up to $5, also costing $10 each. Books must have at least a 4 star rating.

theereadercafe.com - listing 99c books in exchange for a like on Facebook.

Bookbub – One of best promotion sites but expensive depending on your book price and genre. You must be accepted before you are allowed to promote on this site.

worldliterarycafe.com - running '99c Fridays'. It costs $20 to participate.

indiesunlimited.com – offering 'Thrifty Thursdays' for 99c books.

addictedtoebooks.com - accepting free submissions of books costing up to $5.99. Your book must have at least five reviews.

Kindle Nation Daily – offering a range of pay-for services for authors.

digitalbooktoday.com - selling a variety of services for authors.

Thekindlebookreview.net – sells a variety of services for authors. Freebooksy – your book must be priced between 99 cents and $5.

UK

Indie Book Bargains - accepting books priced up to £2.99. Follow instructions.

flurriesofwords UK - offering some cheap paid promotions for bargain books. .

hotukdeals.com - allowing you to list discount books.

bookbargainsuk.com - offering paid promotional opportunities.

FACEBOOK:

Ebookpromos – List your Countdown Deals here.

KindleDailyDeals – Lists all kindle deals. Be sure to follow forum rules.

NookandKindleEbookDeals – Has a form on site for all ebook deals.

KindleCountdownDeals – Open group, make sure to follow forum rules.

Ereader News Today – Lists bargain books.

Twitter:

@EbookCountdown

@KindleDailyDeal

@kindledeals

@freebookpromos

@CrazyKindle

@AllKindleDeals

@KindleDeals

@ShopKindleDeals

Other sites:

Goodreads – You can list your bargain books here but you must be a member of Goodreads

Kindle User Forums – Go to both the US and UK sites – follow forum rules

US

UK

Also don't forget to promote on your own blog and social media sites!

Kindle Unlimited Membership:

Amazon just rolled out a new program called Kindle Unlimited – a $9.99 monthly subscription plan that allows customers to explore over 600,000 titles and thousands of audiobooks with unlimited reading and listening. Consumers also get a 30-day free trial.

So what does that mean for authors?

Here's how it works:

Authors already enrolled in Kindle Direct Publishing (KDP Select) will also be included in the Kindle Unlimited list of books. That means more potential to get your work into reader's hands. And yes you get paid.

It can be a bit confusing.

According to Amazon, here's how it should work:

FOR CONSUMERS: U.S. Amazon Prime members who own Kindle devices will get to choose from thousands of books to borrow for free through the Kindle Owner's Lending Library. Included on the book list are more than 100 New York Times Bestsellers. Readers get to check out one book a month with no due date. Now customers can get unlimited reading plus audiobooks for a $9.99 monthly subscription under Kindle Unlimited.

Learn more about Amazon Prime at www.amazon.com/kindleprime, or find additional details on eligibility at www.amazon.com/help/kindleownerslendinglibrary.

FOR AUTHORS: Writers must agree to publish their digital book exclusive to Amazon for 90 days. This enrolls the author's book title into Kindle Direct Publishing. In return the author has the ability to off his book for free for five days of the 90. Authors also get to do time-bound sales and get compensated when their titles are borrowed from the Kindle Owner's Library.

The addition of Kindle Unlimited adds another royalty possibility for authors.

Authors currently receive a percentage from a KDP Select fund – usually $2 per title borrowed. Under Kindle Unlimited, authors will be paid in the same manner. The desire would be that your book get borrowed through both programs – increasing your profit per title.

Amazon is still testing this subscription service and how titles are enrolled or who gets paid is still fuzzy but Indy authors should take advantage of any platform made available for more visibility. And here's two ways you can make more money using these forums.

MARKETING IDEAS: Amazon allows prime membership gifting. So you can purchase and give loved ones a $99 annual membership for a special occasion or as a holiday gift. Many authors use rafflecopter **(more on this in Chapter 11)** or other services to promote book or Kindle Fire giveaways on their website. Why not a prime membership? You could use it to promote your Kindle Books, your website or social media accounts.

Along with your regular book promotions, earn income advertising the Amazon free reading application: Starting June 16, 2014 Associate Program affiliates became eligible to earn $1 for every new Kindle Reading App signup on both desktop and mobile devices.

The FREE Kindle reading app lets your customers read their favorite books on most devices (PCs, smartphones, tablets, etc.), and creates an opportunity for you to increase your eBook commissions as your customers find more occasions to read.

See the Associate Program Operating Agreement [https://affiliate-program.amazon.com/gp/associates/agreement] and Associates Program Advertising Fee Schedule [https://affiliate-program.amazon.com/gp/associates/help/operating/advertisingfees] for complete terms.

Tip: Once you are an Associate you can grab banners and links from the Amazon site and embed it into your websites. You can also promote it on your social media forums.

$.99 Kindle Deals:

The $.99 price point for ebooks continues to be a hot topic among authors. Some writers have embraced the concept while other writers still refuse to sell their digital titles at this price. Like any marketing plan, the results are dependent on many variables: timing, publicity, consumer wants and product quality. Still, we believe authors need to take advantage of all promotional programs available. If you don't want to price your ebooks at $.99, don't. But don't close the door on it entirely. You can still use 99 cent pricing as a marketing strategy.

Before we get into all that, let's take a look at the pros and cons of the inexpensive digital sale.

Advantages:

Most buyers are willing to risk $.99 for a book even if they don't know the author

If you have other titles, the $.99 book could draw readers to your other work

There are many sites where you can advertise your $.99 titles so they're easier to pitch than higher priced books.

You could increase book sales.

Digital books don't cost you printing or shipping costs, so every sale is profit.

Disadvantages:

You don't make as much of a royalty because Amazon only pays 35 percent royalty on books priced under $2.99. Books priced $2.99 or higher receive 70 percent royalty. So you would have to sell more books at 99 cents than you would for books priced at $2.99 or higher.

Your book may have a lower perceived value by readers.

How to use 99 cent deals for marketing:

- Use your promotion to advertise a series or other books you've written. For example, writer and blogger Molly Greene wanted to wait until she had three published novels in place before pitching her fiction series. So to launch her new book, *Paint Me*, she ran a two week $.99-sale for the first book in her series, *Mark of the Loon*.

95

She submitted her sale to a number of no-cost ebook deal websites that advertise discounted books at no charge. On the second week, Molly submitted her sale to low-cost sites spending a total of $20.

Molly said she saw a boost in sales for all the books in her series. Read her full blog post, including a listing of sites she used for her promotion: Molly Greene: Writer.

- Some authors have made their books permanently free. Instead of sales, these writers are seeking to brand themselves and build a following for future books. Why not do the same with a 99 cent title and instead of making zero profit, you can make some revenue while positioning yourself. We sold our ebook marketing title, *Sell more Ebooks – how to increase sales and Amazon rankings using Kindle Direct Publishing* at $.99 for several months, landing us on several top 20 category lists. In addition, we earned many positive reviews and increased our following at Kindle Book Promos – a site dedicated to the promotion of authors and their books.

We used several ebook deal websites – using both free and paid promotions. In addition, we ran Rafflecopter giveaways offering entrants Amazon Gift Cards as prizes. Anyone that bought a copy of our book received 10 extra entries in the Gift Card giveaway.

We will discuss how to use Rafflecopter in more detail in Chapter 11.

- Some writers have made a living writing several books and pricing each at $.99. If you go to Amazon's top 100 paid bestsellers, you'll see at least a dozen books by some lesser-known authors on the list. When you click on these author profiles, some of them have an entire list of $.99 books all on top seller paid lists. Many of these authors are making a six-figure income. Why not you?

Places to list your 99 cent promos – these sites also have high-ranking Alexa which means you the potential to reach a higher number of readers when you list or advertise on these blogs.

Kindle Book Promos – free and paid promotions available.

Bookbub – pricey and you must be approved to list but if you have the right type of book, big sales are possible.

Bargain Booksy – Not as pricey as Bookbub but more costly than other sites. Still, a nice platform for promoting.

Ereader News Today

Many Books

Kindle Nation Daily

The Kindle Book Review

Book Daily

EbookHunter

Book Goodies

Awesomegang

The Independent Author Network

GoodKindles

Daily Free ebooks – Don't let the site name fool you, the forum no longer is a free ebook promotion service. Dedicated to books costing 99 cents or less.

Pixel of Ink – Brisk traffic. Be sure to post at least 30 days out.

The following three sites are also high-ranking Alexa blogs but you have to be a member or pay for advertising to take advantage of the premium features available. We have used all three in the past with success. In addition we are members and affiliates of The Author Marketing Club.

The Author Marketing Club – Must be a premium member to use all the great marketing tools, such as book description formatting software for Kindle, which creates an appealing list of your books and converts it to a widget for your blog. This forum also offers free marketing videos and many other helpful applications. The cost is around $100 for one year or you can pay month to month at a higher annual fee.

Note: A basic membership is free. You don't have access to all the cool tools but you still get some great benefits: A forum to list your books for reviews, a tool to submit your free days to several promotion sites and access to many affordable advertising opportunities. We recommend you take advantage of this site.

World Literary Cafe – This is a great site and if you haven't joined, do so. You'll find opportunities to increase your Twitter and Facebook followings. In addition, the Cafe has twitter teams to help get your tweets to a larger audience – especially helpful when running promotions. The site also has book review, blog requests and book marketing forums.

In addition the site hosts 99 cent Fridays and a slew of other marketing opportunities, including some free options.

Book Tweeting Service – This site has a large audience of active book buyers. On one occasion, we used the service for two days and sold 63 books but during another promotion, we used the service for two days and only sold 12 books. Again, there are no guarantees on book sales, but the service is good and the followers are real people looking for books.

BONUS: Here's a UK site that offers low-cost ads on a newsletter that targets English-speaking markets all over the world. They also list INDY bookstores that have online sites as well as Amazon, Kobo and Barnes & Noble. Here's the link: EbookBargainsUK.

Good Twitter Sites:

https://twitter.com/ebooks99cents

https://twitter.com/99KindlePromos

https://twitter.com/99ebooks

https://twitter.com/KindleSwag

https://twitter.com/CrazyKindle

https://twitter.com/99centsale

https://twitter.com/book_tribe

https://twitter.com/AllKindleDeals

In this next section we are going to talk about book reviews, which still mean a lot to readers and Amazon.

Chapter 10: Book Reviews – how to get your book into the right hands

Book reviews matter; they're the street cred builders for new authors and new releases. Amazon uses book reviews and customer satisfaction ratings as part of their ranking formula for Top 100 lists. Customers use reviews to determine whether they want to buy an item and publishers seeking new talent keep an eye on these statistics as well.

Writers have enough trouble pitching books for sales, now they need to scrounge up reviews as well. Yep. This is part of the process. But you can streamline your efforts by including book review requests as part of your overall marketing plan.

a. Ask for a book review and provide a link for the reader at the end of your published work.
b. If you have the $400 per review from reputable critics like Kirkus or Publisher Weekly, take advantage. You should be aware that most readers today don't put a lot of stock in high-profile reviews. They rely more on what their friends and neighbors – or fellow Romance lovers – are saying. However, book stores, traditional publishers and libraries still use big-name reviews for their evaluations … so if you're targeting these places and have the money, go for it.
c. Include book review requests at the end of blog posts, within author-friendly forums and when possible in your tweets or social media posts.

Blogger, online readers and Social Media

Major news publications continue to shut out INDY authors, even though there were more than 235,000 self-published titles as of 2011. But it hasn't stopped independent writers from getting noticed.

In June 2013, Amazon announced that Oliver Pötzsch, whose Hangman's Daughter series includes *The Hangman's Daughter* (2010), *The Dark Monk* (2012), and *The Beggar King* (2013), had become the first Amazon Publishing author to sell 1 million copies in combined print, audio, and Kindle English language editions worldwide.

Digital Book World (networking resource for consumer publishing professionals and their partners) claims at least ten self-published books were best sellers in 2013. And these authors did it all through online word-of-mouth receiving little, if any, support from major news outlet or others attached to the perceived "monopoly" within the big umbrella of conventional publishing circles. Instead these success stories resulted from online mediums.

So put them to your own use.

First Steps:

- Have pristine PDF, mobi and print copies available for potential reviewers.

- While a sales sheet or press kit may be required by some readers, most online reviewers are satisfied with a copy of your book and a sales sheet that should include your ISBN, genre, book price, sales page links, brief author bio and contact information.

- Draft a cover letter consisting of author info, a blurb about the book (60-100 words) and a request for a book review. Keep it short, to the point and professional. Don't pester the reviewer. A one-time follow-up is reasonable if you haven't heard back after two or three weeks. After that, if you don't hear from the reviewer, move on.

- Have enough copies on hand to cover the requests. It looks unprofessional to contact someone who replies with an OK and then make them wait for your book.
- Budget accordingly as you may have to gift some books, mail print books or ship from a distributor. You should also consider any extra advertising costs to get the word out: Facebook Ads, sites that charge fees – most authors use Rafflecopter or Goodreads to announce book giveaways, running an ad on giveaway sites or even on Goodreads is a good way to get the word out.

Tips for getting book reviews:
- Target reviewers you know are interested in your genre. You'd be surprised how many authors don't take the time to research the right place and person. By the way, you should have a clearer idea of who your target audience is if you have done your category and keyword searches properly. Us that same knowledge to find reviewers.
- Query the reviewers. Each bloggers Amazon reviewer or other book reader has his or her requirements. Some may wish to be queried first. Others prefer hard covers to digital files.
- Be polite and professional. This info covered above so I deleted. When you do get a review, positive or otherwise, thank the person for their time. And if the criticism is valid, learn from it.

At one time, it was unacceptable to buy reviews. Even now, none of the main players, including Amazon, will admit "paid" summaries. But almost every bestselling book has had at least one paid review and though Amazon says it frowns on this practice, it allows paid Kirkus and Publisher Weekly reviews even promoting the practice on Createspace.

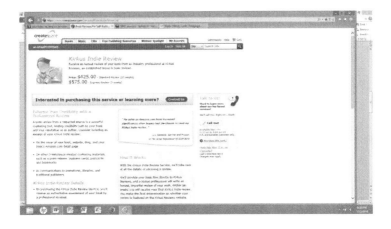

Paid versus Free reviews:

A number of book review services have appeared in response to the ever growing onrush of self-publishers looking quotable evaluations. But you have to be careful. While there are professionals and reputed critics offering reviews for a fee, there are others only interested in taking your money.

Getting attention for your book is difficult if you are an unknown author. But some writers had enough marketing savvy and money to manipulate the system. For example, when INDY icon John Locke, author of, "How I Sold 1 Million eBooks in 5 Months," admitted to buying over 300 reviews to help boost his visibility – he created an outraged backlash.

Locke bought his reviews through a site shutdown due to bogus book reviews, according to a *New York Times* article on the subject. Some in the publishing world are still angry with Locke, others see him as someone who was smart enough to use the system to his advantage.

Fake reviews and other marketing ploys like the above forced Amazon to create new policies. However, some of the changes were not well publicized, causing a great deal of confusion.

For unspecified reasons, many book reviews disappeared overnight. Some sites were forced to shut down and some authors were actually removed from Amazon's site. Now that the dust has settled, things seem to be running more smoothly.

Here is a clarification: On Amazon, you can gift your book for a review but the reviewer should disclose that fact when posting an evaluation of your work. In addition: "Paid reviews are welcome in the 'Editorial Reviews' section of a book's detail page. Reviews written for any form of compensation other than a free copy of the product are not allowed in the Customer Reviews section."

So whether you pay or not is up to you. A respectable rave could help you with advertising but paid or not, a good review doesn't guarantee sales. If you'd like to investigate further:

- Blue Ink Review - $395 and up
- ForeWord Reviews – Clarion Reviews start at $335 and take up to 8 weeks
- Kirkus Reviews – Start at $425 and takes up to 9 weeks. Other services available
- Your First Review - $149 and includes a 7 point report

Tip: Remember you are paying for an honest review of your work and it's coming from people seasoned veterans. We recommend sticking to free or book-gift reviews which we feel produce better results.

Here's a list of lesser known names in the traditional publishing world that are popular with INDY Authors:

San Francisco Book Review – You do not have to be from San Francisco to submit your book for review. It is free to submit and be considered. For a fee, you are guaranteed a review.

Portland Book Review – You do not have to be from San Francisco to submit your book for review. It is free to submit and be considered. For a fee, you are guaranteed a review.

<u>Book Review Buzz</u> – For $25, you can list your book at this site and your title will be sent to a list of 1,700 readers. If you want a guaranteed book review, the fee is $150.

<u>Verified Book Reviews</u> – This is a paid review service that includes buying your digital book copies, a sale that will boost your rankings. In addition, the review will be listed as a verified buyer on Amazon.

<u>Kindle Book Review</u> – This site offers very affordable prices for book review packages including a premium service that includes the purchase your book to help with sales rankings.

FREE book reviews:

Of course, FREE, is always best but keep in mind you will probably wait longer. Here's a list of the most reputable sites:

<u>Midwest Book Review</u> – Run by good people. There is no charge for print editions and this organization makes its reviews available to libraries.

<u>Kindle Obsessed</u> – Could take up to 3 months for a review but it is free.

<u>The Kindle Book Review</u> – Has a list of reviewers and there is no charge.

<u>The Author Marketing Club</u> – You have to be a member to use the forums on this site, including the book review discussions, but it is free to sign up. In addition, premium members will also receive book marketing tools and instructions.

<u>World Literary Café</u> – You have to be a member but signup is free. This site offers a lot of forums over and above book reviews. In addition, there are a number of free and paid book marketing opportunities including tweet teams.

Goodreads – Recently acquired by Amazon, it is still one of the largest author and reader connected communities online. There are a number of groups that discuss books, review threads and review request forums.

Parapublishing – Dan Poynter offers free newsletters as well as a vast list of services for authors. If you register for his free publishing newsletter, you can list your books for review.

Book Blogger Directory – This site offers a large data base listed in alphabetical order of book bloggers that accept review requests.

BookReviews – This is a relatively new site with book review opportunities and includes an Author Pitch page where writers get 35 words or less to tell readers why they should buy a book.

Now let's take a look at how to market your books online through popular social media sites.

Chapter 11: Social Media and other promo opportunities

In decades past, book promotion relied on the traditional press. But self-published authors don't have that advantage, so we've turned to the Internet to get noticed. Fortunately, there are millions of bloggers who have large audiences and are open to learning about our work. More importantly, this same group can reach others with just one click through Facebook, Twitter and Linkedin.

If you understand the power of these forums and how to make each work for you, you'll sell more books, gain a following and open doors that would have never been secured by a short piece in a newspaper. However, should you get the opportunity to be in any reputable publication, don't pass up the free publicity.

We have found the following suggestions on how to use the top 3 platforms beneficial:

Twitter
Twitter is one of the most popular social sites in the world and there are many ways to tap into the social of this medium. For the time being, we'll focus on basic strategies.

    a. Set-up – Here's where keywords and categories play another key role. When you register for Twitter, you will be asked for a user name. Some people use their pen name or book title. Since we operate Kindle Book Promos – a site that promotes authors and their books – we use the following Twitter names: @penabook and @freebookpromos. So our customized Twitter URLs are as follows: https://twitter.com/penabook and https://twitter.com/freebookpromos.

You will also be asked for your website URL and a brief description of yourself. Your keywords or category names should have also been used for your domain name and try to include keywords in your brief site description. Ours looks like this when your click on twitter:

Tip: Use nice photos for your profiles that represent you or your site. When you become more Twitter savvy you can also customize your page layout and use other advanced tools. For now, let's keep it straightforward.

b. Creating tweets: Since you're only allowed 140 characters, you'll want to be short, sweet and interesting. This is the time to get the creative juices on BOIL. Believe it or not, with some practice, this process isn't that difficult. Some things to know before starting:

- Hashtags – a word or super-short word group (with no spaces) preceded by a (#) sign to help reach a target audience. For example if you wanted to offer your Romance book for free, you could Tweet: *#Romance on Kindle free today.* (Of course you would include a link for downloading your book.)

- Reply to tweets: Use the symbol @ before the name of the user to whom you're responding. Example: Start your tweet, @username thanks for your kind words.

- URLs: When posting to Twitter you only have 140 characters so don't waste space with a long URL. Shorten your URL using bitly or other similar services.

- Retweets – your goal is to have people Retweet your messages eve as, out of courtesy, you Retweet theirs. You can find who tweeted for you who has been asking for a RT by clicking on @connect – the link next to the Home link right above the box where you type your posts.

If you use RT and the username of the profile you are Retweeting, it should look like this: *RT@penabook See long list of Kindle Freebies today* http://bit.ly/P5duSD

Tip: If you only use 112-115 characters, you'll leave space for RT or another username.

How to use Twitter for Promotion
The best method of advertising your books is, counterintuitively, NOT to talk too much about your books because Twitter is all about interacting and passing along useful or interesting information. While you might find your work fascinating, others may not.

You should try to keep your book promotions to no more than three or four mentions every other day unless you are running a free promotion when people would expect to see more tweets.

Instead, RT books by other authors; reply to questions by twitters in your genre; pass along marketing tips or interesting news articles about writing, book promotion or publishing. Congratulate people on accomplishments. If someone posts an award, tell them how great that is.

If someone is looking for information and you can help them, reply to their tweet.

Make it more about others than yourself and people will start helping you pitch your books, services and messages. Look at it as the largest online network for your work.

How to find the right people:
- Use the Twitter search link to find people you want to interact with who can help you promote your book.

a. Connect with other authors if you want to discuss ideas, writing and other common interests. These are people with similar taste and interests you can follow and have discussions with on a regular basis. If you are a History writer, you can do a search for *"History Writers."*

b. Look for Key people who can help promote your book: bloggers, reviewers, promoters. These are people you can contact through their websites to see if they have services you might be looking for. In addition, you can keep an eye out for their needs. If a blogger is looking for authors to interview, you should reply. We often send out tweets letting authors with new book releases know they can post their titles on our site for free.

c. Follow Free Book Promoters. We often RT anyone that follows us and tells us about their promotions.

d. Use twitter to make announcements. If you are offering a giveaway, have a featured guest or blog tour to promote, post it on Twitter.

Tip: Balance your promotion-centric tweets with plenty of Retweets, @ replies and original tweets. Offering new and interesting information and make your promotions intriguing.

- Use Twitter to find book buyers.

a. There are readers on Twitter that request #Kindlesuggestions #bookstoread. Often, when someone is taking their new Kindle on a trip, they'll post that they are looking for good books. Sometimes you'll be given specific genres or author names. If your book fits this category, reply and tell them about it.

b. Sometimes during the holidays, there are groups looking for books to send to classrooms, troops stationed overseas or natural disaster victims. After Hurricane Katrina, we answered the call of a tweet classrooms needing educational books. Most often the books sent to these groups would be free or sold at a large discount. We enjoy this activity and we have received some fabulous reviews in the process.

- Brand Yourself

a. Twitter is a great place for nonfiction writers, especially if you write how-to or self-help books. Since most authors are looking for book marketing ideas, what better way to promote your book about marketing than offering a tip or two online and sending people to a page where your book is offered.

This is one of our running tweets:
Winner of Global Ebook Award for Marketing: Sell more Ebooks only $2.99 on Kindle - http://amzn.to/1741TkV

Here's another one:
Learn how to increase sales and Amazon rankings, only $2.99 http://amzn.to/1741TkV

But it doesn't have to be a promotion like ours. You can tweet something like this: Don't forget Black Friday is the biggest shopping day. Other tips: http://amzn.to/1741TkV

You can also offer free webinars, twitter chats and other marketing strategies to announce to your following at Twitter.

Health writers might offer diet tips or exercise ideas in their tweets and then link to their sales page with books, products and other related information.

- Find "influencers" – Research key players in your niche and find out what they are working on. When we published our first marketing book, *Sell More Ebooks*, one of the people we came across online was Anthony Wessel. It was a chance meeting in a discussion about parents and travel. Anthony wrote a book, *One Minute Washington D.C. Travel Stories,* about a trip he took with his 85-year-old dad. In our email exchanges we agreed to review his book. When *Sell More Ebooks* was published, we contacted him for an endorsement which he agreed to.

What we didn't know at the time is that Anthony is the founder of Digital Book Today and The Top 100 Best Free Kindle Book List which is updated daily. Anthony is a book industry veteran, having worked with Borders/Waldenbooks and Egghead Software. Over time, he has become very helpful for us with both free and paid promotions that spurred our book to bestseller status, #1 in two separate categories. We continue to use Anthony's services and highly recommend his website. He is a great guy.

The point is that these type of mutually beneficial relationships can be priceless.

Tip: Reach out to influencers on Twitter and see what you can do to help THEM. For instance, if your niche expert has a free webinar, offer to post about it on your website or Facebook page. Or maybe they are seeking a service you offer. Be open to opportunities.

Influencer and book marketing expert, Tom Corson-Knowles suggests the following:

"The best time to connect with busy people on Twitter is Sunday around 9 a.m. That's when busy executives and business people have some time to catch up." – from his book, *How to Make Money with Twitter: A Complete Guide To Twitter Marketing And Monetization (Get More Twitter Followers And Make More Sales Online With Social Media, Sell More, Web Traffic)*.

Keywords: The importance of our old pals, keywords, never ends. Throughout your social media conversations, beginning with your user name and carrying right on up tp and through your messages, make use of your keywords and categories. Whenever possible, plug them into all your headings and conversations cunningly, without sounding like you're speaking a foreign language.

When tweeting, use words that describe your genre, category, audience or website.

Twitter Tools:

There are a variety of twitter tools available depending on your needs. We however, recommend you invest in at least one of those listed below.

TweetAdder – This is one of the best Twitter marketing software available and at a great cost. If you are just learning twitter and have only one account, purchase the personal package. If you plan on expanding or already have a publishing business, we advise purchasing the 10-account deal. This software is easy to use and to set up. It is as helpful for beginners as it is for advanced users.

Hootsuite – This is an easy setup for beginners and the basic services are free. We use this when promoting our free day or discounted books. It allows you to set up multiple tweets and to schedule them in advance.

Socialoomph – This is perhaps the best known service and has evolved into a multi-tasking twitter operation. If you are a beginner, this site may be confusing or overwhelming but you can explore and test its benefits for free. Advanced users can purchase a professional setup with additional features. Two of the most popular benefits of this site are that you can set up a welcome message to your twitter followers and you can schedule tweets in advance.

You will also want to use a link reducer – these are two of the most used on Twitter:

http://tinyurl.com/
https://bitly.com/

- Link Reducers or Shorteners condense the length of your urls – remember you only get 140 characters on Twitter.

- Example: Our website is http://kindlebookpromos.luckycinda.com After we plug it into bitly, it becomes http://bit.ly/1l4uoRz. We now have 15 additional characters for our marketing message. In tweet language that is a lot.

Putting it all together

BEGINNERS: If this is your first time on Twitter or you are fairly new to the platform, here are some tips:

- Define your market: Who are you trying to communicate your message to, romance readers, book bloggers, other writers? Knowing your audience will help you come up with targeted messages. Remember to use hashtags for your target reader: #writers, #readers, ect.

- Speak to your reader and always offer value ... don't just send out messages about your book. For example, if you have written a Romance and want to interact with readers of that genre, you might post questions for them that don't have to do with selling your book. You might send something like this: What makes someone sexy on a page? I always ask when writing romance. #readers #writers

  If someone responds, interact. To do so, just hit the reply button below their tweet.

  Other messages can be links to romance book blogs, book marketing tips for authors or news items that pertain specifically to your audience. Now and then you can mention your book but if and when you do, try to make it interesting don't just say buy my book!

- Build a following. Some people will begin following you based on your interest or your tweets. But you can also build a following by becoming active with others. A quick way to do so would be to help others spread their message by retweeting. Find a tweet you like or that is interesting and hit the retweet button under the message. A lot of people will return the favor and RT one of your messages. You can also follow people. Some will automatically follow back.

Note: As you become more comfortable, implement your twitter tools.

ADVANCED MARKETING:
NEW for 2014 and 2015 – Twitter has added a lot of new tools this year. You can now make your profile pages stand out with professional-looking backgrounds and personal images. In addition, you can insert videos and images into your tweets. Like Facebook, you can now highlight tweets that will be posted at the top of your account page.
Twitter is still experimenting with advertising but you can currently buy targeted tweets and choose who to target with your message. The jury is still out on how effective this is but it is another opportunity for those with a budget to spend.

For the Twitter savvy: We like to use applications allowing "follow buttons" on social media sites like Wordpress and Facebook and we also like to host contests, surveys and polls. Apps allow you to post and link these activities on all your social media sites.

Once you are all "linked" up, you can try these Twitter Marketing ideas:

a. **Twitter Party:** An online event. Parties take typically 1 to 2 hours and can be about any topic. We have used Twitter Parties to discuss book marketing ideas and as a thank you venue to followers during which we gave

116

away free books to people on our follow list. One of our authors used a Twitter party as a Q&A about her book.

How does it work? Twitter users are given a Hashtag (#) prior to the party. On the day of the event, users search for the hashtag word, like #bookmarketingparty, to follow the event.

Make the party fun. Offer prizes. Try to have a set schedule so you build a following. Some authors like to host weekly parties, others do it monthly and you can also use it for special events only – like a book launch. Be creative – the possibilities are many.

The easiest way to host or join a twitter party conversation is through Tweetdeck, Tweetchat or Tweetgrid.

We promote our Twitter Parties through word of mouth by posting about it on our website, Facebook, email list and Twitter. On the day of the party, we use Tweetchat to communicate with our audience. If you build a large following, it is helpful to have a facilitator for the event. If you need help with promotion or hosting, there are some good services available. Here are two we recommend:

- **Twitter Party Guide** - $25 to promote your party and $5 to list on their party calendar – Read Details

- **Mommy Blog Expert** – Great site with all the information you need to get your party started. This site also lets you post your party free on their calendar. Read Details

b. **Giveaways** – We love Rafflecopter which gives you easy tools to set up contests and giveaways.

There are three reasons we use this type of service for promotion:

- To increase visitors to our website. We can use Twitter as a communication tool to let followers know that if they visit our website, they can enter to win some type of prize. Usually we offer Amazon gift cards or books.

- To advertise our books. With Rafflecopter you can have readers retweet your messages for extra entry points in your giveaways. Not only is this free advertising for your book, it allows you to host book giveaways apart from the Kindle Select Book Giveaways that limit you to five-day promotions within a 3-month window.

- To make money. We charge $10 for anyone who wants to host or advertise their own giveaways at our site: Kindle Book Promos. This is a win-win since we and the advertiser get increased exposure to our links.

c. **Mentoring** – Twitter is a great place to meet people. If you offer any type of book or publishing service, Twitter's platform is a free community where you can tell others about your expertise. For example, sometimes people have questions about book marketing. Since we do a lot of that, sometimes we go on Twitter and, through hashtags or chat forums looking for questions we can answer. You could it every day, once a week or schedule it monthly. Sometimes, we give free books to people on our follow list just to say thank you for following us. Because we're offering something for nothing, more people are willing to help us and get the word out when it comes our turn to advertise a book or event.

Don't forget to use twitter teams, tribes or forums that help with retweets.

World Literary Café
The Author Marketing Club
Triberr
Goodreads
Message us:
@penabook
@freebookpromos
@99KindlePromos
@EbookCountdown
EbookPromos

Now let's take a look at Facebook.

Facebook

Facebook has become another mega online giant but most small purveyors don't know how to take advantage of it. Think of it as an ultra-social party where people exchange photos, personal information and even have conversations back and forth that would make grandma cringe … but since she is also probably on Facebook … well.

So let's get back to the party. The last thing you want to do is try to run driving business chat into the middle of a conversation about who got inebriated last night. To avoid the personal hoopla and sidestep the social land mines, it is important to create a business page that is separate from your personal account.

Facebook Setup:
a. Before you set up a business page you'll need to create a profile on Facebook.

1. Go to Facebook and register by providing the required information.

2. Invite your friends, Twitter contacts and email contacts to connect with you – Facebook gives you an option to add your email contacts automatically. While this idea makes some wary, Facebook will only add the people on your contact list that are already on Facebook. Happily, you also have the option to pick and choose.

3. You can now write your first post.

b. Fan Page – This is a template under your profile that will be used as your business page.

1. Go to www.facebook.com/pages and click "Create your own" at the top right of the page.
2. Pick the type of page that best relates to your business and fill in the information.

Tip: As usual, keywords and categories come into play. When picking a "company name." use your book title, logo or book sub-title. If you offer services like book marketing, use that in your title too. We call our Facebook page ebookpromos.
Your name is important as it will show up whenever you post or when others share your content or mention your fan page.

3. Pick a professional image. We suggest using your publicity photo or book cover.

4. Fill out the About section: And guess WHAT? Since it will be indexed by Google, **USE your KEYWORDS**.

c. Advanced Setup – Upload a Timeline Cover that must be 851 x 315 pixels. Next go to "Edit Page Setting," and click on "Update Info." Fill out as much information as pertains to your site. Don't forget to include a link to your book website.

d. Once your Fan Page is up and running, click "Like" on your fan page. Next, invite your friends by clicking "Build Audience."

Note: Don't invite people that are not interested in your business even if they are 20-year friends – keep the personal and professional photos, comments and conversations separate. When starting out, spread the word about your Fan Page and attempt to get people you don't know to "Like" the page. These will be sincere fans of your information.

Once you have 25 fans, Facebook will allow you to pick a unique URL for your Fan Page.

e. One last trick: Click on "About Section" of your profile and click "Edit." Now go to the "Where did you work?" box and type in the name of your fan page and click it. When people go to your profile and click on the link, it will automatically take them to your Fan Page.

Why Fan Pages Matter:

Marketing on Facebook

Although Facebook is an interactive community, you are obviously not limited to 140 characters. On Facebook, it's easier to upload photos, videos and even whole templates. Please be aware of and abide by all anti-spam policies and professional protocols.

Once again, we've discovered that the best way to build a following is to offer services, products and advice people want. You build trust when you share and exchange with like-minded people. If you do too much selling, you run the risk of being declared a "spammer," which means you'll be blocked from certain groups ... or even from Facebook itself.

Note: When searching for groups to follow don't look for more than three or four every other day. Otherwise Facebook will block you block you temporarily thinking you are only seeking places for your sales pitch.

Best Facebook Practices:

a. Join relevant Facebook groups – if you write mysteries, find other mystery authors, readers or mystery clubs.
b. Create polls with interesting or funny topics.
c. Share free giveaways.
d. If you are a nonfiction writer, use Facebook as a hub of advice.
e. Promote your own products once every other day on your site.
f. When you have a FREE day giveaway, only post once a day unless you have permission to do otherwise.
g. Be professional and courteous.

Facebook Tools:

a. Get a Like Box – the best method for building a fan base:
   developers.facebook.com/docs/reference/plugins/like-box

b. Get a like or follow button for your website. If you use Wordpress, look for social media plugins.

c. To build template pages such as bookstores, sales sites or other pages you need as part of your Fan Page, use http://pagetabapp.com/

BEGINNERS: If you are new to Facebook, you might want to join a group or two of people with similar interests. This will give you an idea of how people communicate on Facebook:

Go to the group you want to be part of and then click **Join Group** in the top right corner. You can also join any Open group that you see on the "about page" of someone's Timeline by clicking **Join**.

You may have to wait for a group administrator to approve your request. In some groups, you can be added by a friend who's already a member.

How to build a following:

On Facebook, although you can only friend people you know, you can like any page you come across. Since our Facebook page is about book promotions, Ebookpromos, we try to like similar Facebook sites. Usually the site owners like us back or their readers do after posting information on our site. This is a quick method of building an audience.

As we discussed with Twitter, you'll build the right brand by providing interesting content to your readers. This might consist of fun photos, interesting quotes, publishing information or interacting in an ongoing conversation.

Once you feel comfortable with Facebook you can opt into other marketing ventures.

ADVANCED MARKETING:

NEW for 2014 and 2015 – Facebook has made a lot of changes to its pages and probably will continue to do so in 2015. At times it can be confusing because, while they have strict rules for users, Facebook owners don't think twice about using your information to advertise even without your permission. Their opinion is that you gave your consent when you signed up.

But since it is and will continue to be one of the most visited and used forums online, take advantage of it. We spoke earlier about

Fan Pages. Here are some tips for drawing readers to those pages:

- Think of your cover photo as an ad – use an eye-catching image, hopefully one that conveys the message or product you are pitching.

- Add videos – especially if you are providing a service like book marketing.

- Use Applications to add contests, links and information.

- Use feeds – remember the social media buttons – because they make it easy for people to link in and out of your site.

- Offer something besides your own products – host chats, giveaways, promote for others.

Facebook Contests: Contests attract viewers. Remember, while selling is the goal, it's not the method. Interaction, consumer benefit and emotional connections are backdoor sales tools.

People are attracted to Facebook Cyber love contests and giveaways. Use these to your benefit. Here are some ideas for direct book promotion:

a. Host a Book Cover contest. Tell readers you are having trouble choosing a good cover for your book because you want to characterize the story as an adventure novel – or whatever your genre. You can then provide an excerpt about your book, its cost and purchase link along with the original cover. Have readers submit new cover ideas for your book – doesn't have to be an image, just an idea. You could offer the person with the winning idea an autographed copy of your book.

Follow-up – in this case, it would seem natural to offer a follow-up event. Host a survey with a list of your new cover options and have people vote on which one seems best. Have a random drawing and give away a $10 Starbuck Gift Card offered right on Facebook.

Bonus: You might actually discover a better cover idea!

b. Indirect book promotion events: Say you wrote a book about your dog but you want to engage people and attract new visitors to your site that need not necessarily be book buyers. You could host a photo contest for dog owners who look most like their pets with your readers choosing your winners. You could give your book away to the winner and also have a random drawing for those who voted.

Tip: Here are 2 FREE services that can help set up your promotions: tabsite and Static IFrame.
Facebook has strict rules about this and prefer you use what is known as "Tabs" on your Fanpages.

Rafflecopter: This is an easy tool to use. Automated features include email capture, contest template, scheduling and picking winners at random. (We use this application for all our giveaways.) Annually on our site Kindle Book Promos, we offer both a Black Friday Special and a Christmas Drawing with Kindle products and ebooks as prizes. Rafflecopter allows us to set up the template with our unique contest entry terms.
Using our giveaways as examples, we usually require either a Retweet of our event, a Facebook Fanpage Like, or a blog comment on our site. This activity boosts our page rank on Google too.
Many book promotion sites use these giveaways to feature sponsors. We charge a small fee (between $25 and $50) to link other authors' books as sponsors alongside the Giveaways. Each title gets a blurb and is seen by hundreds of people signing up to win prizes. As of July, 2014, our site averages about 15,000 visitors a month. Last year our Christmas giveaway netted more than 25,000 entries.

In addition, we promote our giveaways at major promotion listing sites.
Rafflecopter is free: http://www.rafflecopter.com/

We also recommend signing up with major giveaway listing sites:
List your Blog Giveaway – also offers to do it for you for small fee.
Blog Giveaway Directory

For more Facebook Contests Information:
Facebook Contests: How to get your Fans Excited
Book Marketing Makeover: Using Social Networks and Facebook Contests to Sell Books

Facebook Groups – Why not start your own? If you have a topic of interest like book marketing, romance writing, publisher tips or anything of that sort, people will come to your site to ask questions and to read other comments. If your group is engaging enough, you will not have to invest a lot of time.
Here's how it works:
Set up a Facebook Group – go to www.facebook.com/groups/ then click +Create Group at the top right and following directions.

Invite people to join like other authors you know or people who are already members of your fan pages. You can also message about the group on Twitter or other social media, including your blogs.

Keep the site "clean" and moderate regularly – delete spam, respond to reader questions, add content of value or have someone else do it for you.

Book Promotion on LinkedIn

The two most important marketing weapons for authors are the profile and status updates.

a. Profile – Along with the required information, LinkedIn allows you to use profile applications that if used properly give FREE advertising. The good news is that these applications are also free.

1. Download applications to your profile by clicking "More" on the top toolbar and then clicking on "Get more Applications." Pick the ones that will help you promote the most easily and offer the most for your audience.

   "Reading List" is an application by Amazon and one we recommend for authors. When filling out your profile, pay attention to the "Publications" section – this is where your reading list will be posted. Add your books here. This will give you exposure on your profile as well as on your network.

b. Status updates – This is where you can post anything NEW about yourself or your products. For instance, you have a new book release, you won an award, your company added a new employee, your book title became a bestseller or you were mentioned in the news.

Your own group – Like Facebook, LinkedIn will allow you to create your own group. Keep in mind that this site is business oriented. So instead of marketing books, you will want to explain the business of marketing books. You might want to talk about the publishing world – the pros and cons of self-publishing, how to find book distributors, how to market to retailers if you are an unknown and other topics of that nature.

Best Practices:
Like Twitter and Facebook, when using LinkedIn, you want to look for opportunities to help others. Answer questions that relate to the topic of your book. Provide helpful information.

Don't misrepresent yourself and don't go on the prowl trying to drop sales copy about your products. Be genuine with your assistance and your data.

In general, be active, positive and helpful and you will be rewarded in the long-run for your efforts.

Other Social Media Marketing ideas:

One of the most obvious media stages for self-promotion would be the Amazon Author Profile at Author Central yet, this is one of the most neglected marketing tools.

Did you know that your name is part of your product? Once you publish a book at Amazon, your name is linked to your book and product page so web surfers can simply do a search for your name. You should embrace this visibility and make it work for you. By using the tools at Author Central at Amazon, you can offer complete strangers a sense of who you are, what other titles you have penned, services you might offer and any other information you want to share: upcoming book signings, promotion trailers, your social media links or when your next book launch is slotted. One of the coolest tools at Author Central is the author discussion forum where writers can engage in a conversation with readers.

Believe it or not, many authors don't have any information about themselves or their services beyond the title and the price of the book. How frustrating might it be when someone wants to reach you for an interview, has questions about your book or wishes to schedule you for an event. Think of the potential sales and free publicity you miss out on by not providing any information about yourself.

People like interaction. If someone feels connected to you, more likely he or she will buy your book. But don't just signup at Author Central. Make it work for you.

Amazon Author Central

First Steps: Go to http://authorcentral.amazon.com/ and enroll. (Yes, Amazon makes you go to a different site to set this up, you can't do it from your KDP Select account. Don't even ask!)

Note: Do not edit BOOK DESCRIPTIONS through Author Central – there is a glitch that makes Author Central override your KDP Select account's book descriptions which would be a nightmare. So, AVOID BOOK DESCRIPTION EDITS.

But DO take advantage of the following features:
- Author biography and photo – be professional. Use this space to offer more details about your background than your KDP account or book cover allows.
- From the Author – Use this feature to tell readers why you wrote the book or share something about your plot or characters … without giving away your story! You have 8000 characters; use them strategically and include keywords.
- Blog Links – you will also be allowed to list your Twitter, Facebook and LinkedIn accounts and each time you post to those platforms, it will update automatically to your Author Central Profile
- Event Dates and Video – Update your event calendar with book signings, online appearances, speaking engagements. You can also add videos like a book trailer or mention additional activities that pertain to your book or services. For example, if you write book marketing titles, this would be a great place to upload book Save the Date notices about marketing webinars, classes or Youtube videos you have created.
- Unique Author Profile URL – Amazon gives you the option to customize your Author Profile URL – ideally you should use the same name you use for your other social media listings.

- Books – List all your books here and don't forget to include editorial reviews, endorsements or your own notes to the reader. DON'T EDIT your BOOKS here. Use your KDP account.

Author Central is a fabulous place for you to advertise yourself, product or service for free. Use it wisely.

Note: You will have to create a separate Author Central page using these same steps for your accounts in other countries. You can use Google Translate to update information on foreign platforms where you don't know the language.

Guest Blogging

There are many blogs willing to print your content if your information is interesting and beneficial to its readers. Our blog, Kindle Book Promos, features bestselling authors who took the time to respond to an email interview. We use their content is used to help other authors with writing, publishing and book marketing ideas. Kindle Book Promos also features a section under Author Tools made up of content submitted to our site that pertains to online marketing.
There are several blog online like ours and all need fresh content. Book Review and Reader blogs are created daily and the newer ones, especially, need author interviews or books to feature.

How to find places to guest post
1. Determine your target audience. What is it you have to offer? An author interview? A book excerpt? Writing or marketing advice? Information on services relevant to the blog's readership?

2. Find blogs with your target audience.
   a. Go to Google and type in your search. For example, if you are a Romance author seeking book reviews, you would look for sites to review your book. Or

you would search for Romance Bloggers where you could post about Romance writing.

b. After you click the search button, click on the upper right button on the right of your screen that looks like a mechanical gear. In the drop box, click on "Search Settings."

c. Scroll to where it says "Results per Page" and scroll the white square box sitting on the number 10 to 100. You are now ready to find blogs looking for your content.

Tip: You can also find places seeking content through your networks on Twitter, LinkedIn and Facebook. If you are properly engaged at these forums, opportunities will become available. For instance, you'll come across people requesting content for on their site or blogs that need author interviews. In addition, look for discussions with topics you are familiar with and offer to write an article for that person appropriate for their audience.

3. Contact blogs that have good traffic and seem to be a nice fit for you. The best method of correspondence is through the blog's contact form. Be sure to read submission guidelines before making a query.

Also see the following:
Authors sharing how they sold books using social media
Creative Marketing Ideas from 10 Great Thought Readers

As you can see, book marketing is a full-time occupation. Find the tools that work best for your promotional needs. Once you've found one or two things that work well, stick with them until they cease to work. AND BE HONEST WITH YOURSELF ... do what you can without making yourself nutso.

Our advice is to automate as much as possible, outsource if you can afford to do so, and be creative. Now let's take a look at our bonus chapter with how book marketing may look in 2015.

131

BONUS CHAPTER

Chapter 12: BONUS CHAPTER - Looking ahead

New technology will continue to alter online sales promotions. Even if you go with a traditional publisher, digital books will continue to outsell printed versions. In fact, over 60 percent of Barnes and Noble sales are digital.

This means you need to understand the publishing landscape from start to finish. Currently, it's difficult for self-publishers to find book distributors, retail book buyers or high-brow reviewers who take Indie authors seriously. But this attitude is changing even as we write this so let's press on.

TopRankBlog – a digital marketing site – predicts many current digital tactics will be revamped to accommodate the growing need to create "a common brand experience across the digital experience on and offline." Customers expect to access and consume information across platforms, apps and devices and in order for brands to "be the best answer" wherever buyers are looking, they'll need to figure out what's next and where to focus.

Some of the top experts in the business representing brands like Cisco, IBM, Dell and Google, to name a few, were interviewed for the TopRankBlog.

We recommend you read the article and apply it to your book marketing needs: http://www.toprankblog.com/2014/05/digital-marketing-2015/

NEW direction for AUTHORS:

In the first quarter of 2012, audiobook sales were up 32 percent. Amazon has its eye on this figure and has already rolled out an audiobook publishing site similar to Createspace. We don't know how much this emerging sector will continue to expand but getting in early is always key to anything new.

Currently one of the fastest growing platforms is ACX – an Amazon subsidiary. Everything you need to know about publishing, distribution and royalties can be found at the site. If you already have an audio version, you can also use the forum to find distribution. Those who need to record an audio can audition and/or hire producers.

This site boasts of 4,302 titles open for auditions, 17,900 producers to choose from and 19,915 audiobooks on sale at Audible, Amazon and iTunes.

More Books; less Pages – Authors on Amazon are finding that it is quicker to make money writing by producing more books with less content. Books of 100 pages or less can be sold for .99 to $2.99 and writers can churn 10 to 12 a year will little effort. Even if only one book of each title is sold a day, at the end of the month – and subsequently at the end of the year – profits add up. Of course, you can't compromise quality. Readers still want good information.

Take a look at Western INDY Author Van Holt – he has numerous books in the Western genre, many bestsellers. Here's his Amazon page. (BTW, we're big fans!)

Then there's our favorite non-fiction writer, Dan Poynter, who has made an enviable living out of self-publishing including having his own top notch publishing enterprise.

The list goes on ... why not add your name?

Tip: Find a niche that you like with limited competition and start writing short novels or non-fiction books. Or stick to something you love, like romance, and write a three-book series instead of a 400 page novel. Expand your writing and marketing world and you will accomplish more in less time.

NON-TRADITIONAL Book Sales – This is a topic that doesn't get as much coverage as it should but we believe it's worth exploring. There are a variety of places that will buy your books like specialty shops, museums, corporations and nonprofit groups to name a few. Getting a foot in the door is the toughest part so working with a book distributor will help.

Since this is a lengthy topic, we'll list some people we work with that we trust. Be sure to tell them author Laura Dobbins sent you ... In some cases you may even get a discount!

Brian Jud – Probably the #1 expert in this field. You can sign up for his services at Book Marketing Works. Brian also offers Book Marketing consultation to any author. If you tell him Laura Dobbins sent you, he will give you a discount but be sure to ask for it before paying.

Association of Publishers for Special Sales – Membership is $89 a year but you get a list of publishers seeking new work. You'll also receive free marketing tips and access to numerous experts in the business like book distributors, buyers and marketers. As a member you're eligible for large discounts regarding anything to do with publishing.

American Authors and Publishers Guild – This is a new membership site that assists independent authors with special sales and publishing needs.

The Cadence Group – Can help you with book packaging needs and sound advice on how to make your book sellable to retail store buyers. Best of all, they'll tell you when not to change a thing.

New Shelves Distribution – Tell them Laura Dobbins sent you. This group specializes in sales to libraries, retailers and specialty shops.
TCK – Owned and operated by Tom Corson-Knowles, a respected bestselling author and book marketing expert. His

company is an international publisher specializing in ebooks on Amazon Kindle.

Note: Some of these services are expensive with payment often required in advance. We are not their affiliates and will make no profit from your purchase. And always keep in mind THERE ARE NO GUARANTEED BOOK SALES. However, if you are willing to invest some time, money and equity sweat, if you are willing to learn and grow with the industry, you can be a bestseller.

Content Marketing:

Content marketing will be bigger than ever, social media marketing will require more diversity and image-centric content will rule. These are the top three of seven online marketing trends that will dominate 2014 according to a September 2013 Forbes article by Jayson DeMers, an Search Engine Optimization specialist.

It's also worth noting a simple message on tablets and smartphones will be preferred over in-depth data not available on these devices.

What does this mean for you and me?

- **Content** – People will be seeking quality content on your blogs and website. Quick and easy appears to be the future trend. Make your posts shorter, your instructions easier and your sales item visually appealing.

  Use Internet tools to find out what your target audience is searching, give them the information, products and services they want and you will make more sales.

137

Here's how:

Jayson DeMer offers the following two tips in his article, *11 Places to Find Awesome Content Marketing Ideas* - READ Full Article Here

a. *We've all seen Google's keyword suggestions when entering a keyword phrase. This simple method can lead to great insight into what people search for in your niche. All you need to do is open your web browser, go to Google.com, and start typing your keyword phrase. As seen in the example below, Google will automatically give you suggestions with popular keyword phrases that are relevant to your niche.*

Google | content marketing|
content marketing
content marketing **institute**
content marketing **world**
content marketing **strategy**

When your search is complete, take a look at the related searches section at the bottom of the screen for more suggestions.

Searches related to **content marketing**

content marketing **strategy**   content marketing **jobs**

content marketing **examples**   content marketing **services**

content marketing **definition**   content marketing **seo**

content marketing **agency**   **b2b** content marketing

b. Soovle.com

If you're looking for a faster method to generate keyword ideas, check out Soovle.com. Like Google, Soovle.com provides a list of keyword phrases based on the keyword you type in. The difference is that Soovle.com provides keyword ideas from several websites all at once:

- Google.com
- Amazon.com
- Bing.com
- YouTube.com
- Answers.com
- Wikipedia.com

Social Media – Utilize software and applications to automate as much of your work as possible. There isn't enough time in the day to be involved with every single social site online. Identify what platforms work best for you but don't ignore building a multi-media platform for your business. Even television and news programs are now embracing twitter, online applications and blogging.

Note: Connected devices like tablets and smartphone sales are expected to soar in the next four years. If your blog isn't mobile-friendly, you will be losing sales. Gary Fox, writer, coach, consultant and founder of TribalCafe, has a great article on how to make your website mobile-friendly. His site, overall, is full of online marketing information and how-tos. READ HERE

Image-Driven – Yes, a book will be judged by its cover. Some of the fastest rising social media sites are image-based. One of the most successful has been Pinterest.
Rob Eagar is the founder of WildFire Marketing, a consulting practice that helps authors and publishers sell more books and spread their message like wildfire. He has a great article at Writer's Digest about using Pintrest for book promotions.

139

His five tips:

- Place "Pin It" buttons on your website to let people add a picture of your book covers to their Pintrest profiles.

- Use Pinterest to bring your novels alive by displaying images of settings, history or details within your story.

- Add behind-the-scene photos of your life as an author

- List printable coupons users can redeem when buying your books

- Host a contest.

Read full article for details and other ideas.

Tip: When building your blog, use vibrant, quality, fun images to enhance your text. Don't forget videos and integrate your site with Pintrest to help you diversify your social media presence.

Joint Ventures - This isn't a new concept. But how partnerships are formed in the future may change. As companies downsize and remaining employees are tasked with multiple job duties, consolidation can only become the rule. Authors are discovering that it is more cost-efficient to do the same. By teaming with people driving toward the same goal using similar methods, writers can get more done and expand their visibility. Sharing the spotlight is no longer taboo and it cuts down on the expense bill too.

- A dozen authors price their books at $.99 each. Instead of promoting just one title to 2,000 twitter followers, the writers promote their titles as a package. The message of the day is that interested readers have 12 different books to choose from at a great price for each. Now instead of 2,000 tweet-happy people, the message can be sent to 24,000 people. If each author has an e-mail list,

140

Facebook account and a personal website, you can see how their combined promotion has the potential for reach on a much grander scale than individually. In addition, if they are promoting the package deal as an author event, they can pool their resources to pay for one set of ads instead of 12.

Branching out is hip. As book stores and traditional media continue to shutout INDY authors, they'll turn to other outlets to make book sales.

Special Sales – There are organizations that specialize in selling books as giveaway incentives to corporations and other establishments. These booksellers normally work on commission or for a one-time fee plus a percentage of book sales. This arrangement is really no different than the cut we get from selling at Amazon or Barnes and Noble.

Finding new audiences will become easier since bookstores and distributors only deal in bulk. Say you wrote a book about bike riding. You could target companies that sell bicycles, talk to bike riding clubs or contact bike riding event organizers. Negotiate with them and demonstrate how buying your book benefits them as well as you. If they use your book as an incentive for club membership, fundraiser giveaways or as a gift to new bike buyers, your book could make them appear generous to new customers and/or more memorable, generating great buzz.
The right partner isn't always the obvious one. Think outside the box. This type of selling will help you online and could rid some of us of those old print copies gathering dust in our garages..

Tip: Offering to include a company's logo on the book or inside cover may be helpful. If you use Print on Demand, this would be an easy and inexpensive fix. You could still do it with traditional printing but it would take longer and probably cost more. If you make a 10,000-book sale, then it probably wouldn't matter. If the sale is for only 50 copies, you'll have to determine if it is worth the cos. Keep in mind that most bulk buyers will expect a healthy discount.

Brian Jud, is an expert in Special Sales. Currently he is the Executive Director for APSS – Association for Publishers for Special Sales. To learn more about this program, go to: http://www.spannet.org/.
Brian also offers a number of Special Sales tips free: http://www.bookmarketingworks.com/index.php?pg=articl es.htm

Amy Collins is a speaker, teacher and author. She operates New Shelves Distribution – a company that helps authors distribute books into stores, gift shops, libraries and airports. To learn more about Amy and her company: http://www.newshelves.com

Advanced Marketing Tools for 2015

Automatic Book Review finder, Amazon Description conversion and professional book widgets:

As digital publishing continues to evolve, the tools in the kit become more innovative although the latest technology is usually the most pricey. One of the better programs we have found and are affiliates of, is the Author Marketing Club.
For a small annual fee – between $100 and $200 by the year or through a month-to-month membership - AMC has several tools to help authors sell more books. Two of our favorites are the Amazon description converter and Book Widget maker.

- Amazon description converter – You fill out a form with your book's headline, description and author bio and the application automatically converts it into the professional standout content with the big Orange headlines and bolded subheads. This helps your book literally stand out on Amazon.

- Book Widget maker - lists up to 10 books and gives your listing a professional look including your book price and sales page links. See our sidebar at Kindle Book Promos under "Holiday Giveaway Sponsors" (sometimes under "Bookspotlight" heading) to see a sample.

But the best tool offered at this site is the Reviewer Getter.
This tool automatically finds book reviewers at Amazon that are relevant to your genre. It provides you with their profile page and contact emails. Best of all, it allows you to organize your contact list.

Videos – Using instruction videos has always been popular and these days, YouTube can make anyone an overnight star. But in 2014, free may start fading. A new and thriving video hub is called udemy – an Internet learning and training center.
There are a number of courses at this site, some are free of charge while others cost up to $300. You could make money either through the site's affiliate program or by offering your services at a cost. Signup is free. A step by step process will show you how to organize and upload your necessary material.
As affiliates, we look for courses and respected entrepreneurs to promote. A class we have taken and recommend is Tom Corson-Knowles' *How to become a Bestselling Author on Kindle.*

Tip: Free videos still drive viewership but people got tired of wasting up to 20 minutes of their time to listen to a sales pitch. It makes sense that customers are more interested in quality content that they can apply. A 5 to 10 minute instruction course will still be helpful at your site or a Facebook post but for more in-depth instructions, people prefer webinars or online classrooms. Now that savvy writers have discovered how to profit from personal insights, free won't be as appealing, especially to its creator.

Note to our Readers:

Lucinda Sue Crosby and Laura Dobbins

Dear readers:

We can appreciate how valuable your time and energy are, not to mention the money and attention you invested in his book We appreciate your support and hope many of your questions about this subject have been answered.

The world needs more accomplished writers like you. We wish you every success –

Thanks! Laura and Lucinda Sue

PS: If you enjoyed this book please leave us a review on Amazon.

Here is a list of our other books:

Francesca of Lost Nation – Romance Adventure and winner of five literary awards

The Cancer Club - a crazy, sexy, inspirational novel of SURVIVAL
Selected as a top-ten finalist in the Next Best Fiction Author Contest by Hampton Roads Publishing and Hierophant Publishing

Water in the West: The Scary Truth about our most Precious Resource -
An Environmental Essay

The Adventures of Baylard Bear – a Story about being DIFFERENT -
Poynter Global Ebook Honorable Mention – Children's Fiction

Why is Pookie Stinky? For Ages 4 to 7 Years Old (Book One: "Silly" Puppy Series 1) -
Short Picture Book Written in Rhyme

Sell more Ebooks – How to increase sales and Amazon rankings using Kindle Direct Publishing
Poynter Global Ebook First Place Winner – Marketing and Advertising

About the Authors:

 Lucinda Sue Crosby is an award-winning author and environmentalist. She is a Nashville songwriter, commissioned poet and journalist. Crosby has won numerous honors for her work. To learn more about the author see her Amazon Author Page.

 Laura Dobbins is a former newspaper reporter, page designer and editor. She has won numerous writing awards as an author and journalist. She also operates Kindle Book Promos, a site dedicated to promoting authors and their work.

REFERENCES

Reference Page: Author Tools

DESIGN SERVICES:

http://www.fostercovers.com/
George Foster, an award-winning designer known for many bestselling covers including *Chicken Soup for the Women's Soul.*

https://www.spawn.org/
The Small Publishers, Artists and Writers Network (SPAWN) offers a $100 book design discount to its members.

http://www.logicalexpressions.com/
There are reasonably priced and knowledgeable freelance artists. Most professionals host or have access to a web site that carries examples of covers they've created. You'll have to do some nosing around and you might query on-line author forums.

http://www.bookmarket.com/101des.htm
John Kremer, book marketing expert and bestselling author, has an extensive list of artists at his website.

But if you need to or wish to design the covers yourself, look for royalty-free art or pay someone up front for their photos or graphics. It's less complicated to buy these components outright so you don't have to deal with copyright or use issues later on.

- We recommend http://www.flickr.com/creativecommons/org and www.clipart.com when building your own covers.
- We've also used www.dreamstime.com and Getty Photos.
- Stock.xchng is somewhat limited but all the images are free.

Ebook FORMATING SERVICES:

http://bit.ly/19ymFKP
Amazon provides a long list of ebook converting services .

Fiverr is a great service to seek professional help for $5 but don't just hire the first service you

http://ebook.online-convert.com/convert-to-epub

http://www.epubconverter.org/

http://bit.ly/1dmo7Mj
Amazon KDP now offers plugins, ebook conversion tools and epub creator

ISBN:
http://www.isbn-us.com/
Book Descriptions that Sell (Free Ebook)
http://authormarketingclub.com/members/free-ebook-signup/

AMAZON BOOK DESCRIPTION TOOLS:

http://www.tckpublishing.com/how-to-use-html-to-format-kdp-kindle-book-descriptions/
TLC

http://authormarketingclub.com/
Author Marketing Club – offered to premium members

AMAZON DIRECT PUBLISHING
https://kdp.amazon.com

BLOG TOURS:

Expresso Book Tours – Has a large following, including nearly 3,000 members on Goodreads. Tours usually include 15 blog stops. Prices are reasonable.

Enchanted Book Promotions – Offers several tour options at affordable prices.

Bewitching Book Tours – A good place for Romance books.

Goddess Fish Promotions – Book in advance as this is a popular site with several opportunities to promote your titles.

Orangeberry Book Tours – Has been in the business over 10 years and excels in site management.

Reading Addiction Virtual Book Tours – Very affordable prices for authors.

Sage Book Tours – Author owned and operated. One of our faves!

HOW to USE PINTEREST:

http://www.yourwriterplatform.com/use-pinterest-to-market-book-and-author-brand/

http://www.thebookdesigner.com/

WHERE to LIST GIVEAWAYS:

http://www.rafflecopter.com/

List your Blog Giveaway – also offers to set everything up for you for a small fee starting at $4.99

Blog Giveaway Directory

Fiverr:

We have used these gigs with great success –
Adds your giveaway to 10 top sites for $5
Will post up to 100 Links for $15

https://apps.facebook.com/contests_giveaways/
For Facebook

TWITTER TOOLS:

TweetAdder – This is one of the best Twitter marketing software available and at a great cost. If you are just learning twitter and have only one account, purchase the personal package. If you plan on expanding or already have a publishing business, we advise purchasing the 10-account deal. This software is easy to use and to set up. It is as helpful for beginners as it is for advanced users.

Hootsuite – This is an easy setup for beginners and the basic services are free. We use this when promoting our free day or discounted books. It allows you to set up multiple tweets and to schedule them in advance.

Socialoomph – This is perhaps the best known service and has evolved into a multi-tasking twitter operation. If you are a beginner, this site may be confusing or overwhelming but you can explore and test its benefits for free. Advanced users can purchase a professional setup with additional features. Two of the most popular benefits of this site are that you can set up a welcome message to your twitter followers and you can schedule tweets in advance.
You will also want to use a link reducer – these are two of the most used on Twitter:

http://tinyurl.com/
https://bitly.com/

TWITTER TEAMS:

World Literary Café
The Author Marketing Club
Triberr
Goodreads

Message us:
@penabook
@freebookpromos
@99KindlePromos
@EbookCountdown
EbookPromos

BOOK REVIEWS:

Big-name Paid Review Sites:

- Blue Ink Review - $395 and up
- ForeWord Reviews – Clarion Reviews start at $335 and take up to 8 weeks
- Kirkus Reviews – Start at $425 and takes up to 9 weeks. Other services available
- Your First Review - $149 and includes a 7 point report

Other Paid Review Sites:

San Francisco Book Review – You do not have to be from San Francisco to submit your book for review. It is free to submit and be considered. For a fee, you are guaranteed a review.

Portland Book Review – You do not have to be from San Francisco to submit your book for review. It is free to submit and be considered. For a fee, you are guaranteed a review.

Book Review Buzz – For $25, you can list your book at this site and your title will be sent to a list of 1,700 readers. If you want a guaranteed book review, the fee is $150.

Verified Book Reviews – This is a paid review service that includes buying your digital book copies, a sale that will boost your rankings. In addition, the review will be listed as a verified buyer on Amazon.

Kindle Book Review – This site offers very affordable prices for book review packages including a premium service that includes the purchase your book to help with sales rankings.

Free Book Review Sites:

Midwest Book Review – Run by good people. There is no charge for print editions and this organization makes its reviews available to libraries.

Kindle Obsessed – Could take up to 3 months for a review but it is free.

The Kindle Book Review – Has a list of reviewers and there is no charge.

The Author Marketing Club – You have to be a member to use the forums on this site, including the book review discussions, but it is free to sign up. In addition, premium members will also receive book marketing tools and instructions.

World Literary Café – You have to be a member but signup is free. This site offers a lot of forums over and above book reviews. In addition, there are a number of free and paid book marketing opportunities including tweet teams.

Goodreads – Recently acquired by Amazon, it is still one of the largest author and reader connected communities online. There are a number of groups that discuss books, review threads and review request forums.

Parapublishing – Dan Poynter offers free newsletters as well as a vast list of services for authors. If you register for his free publishing newsletter, you can list your books for review.

Book Blogger Directory – This site offers a large data base listed in alphabetical order of book bloggers that accept review requests.

BookReviews – This is a relatively new site with book review opportunities and includes an Author Pitch page where writers get 35 words or less to tell readers why they should buy a book.

Now let's take a look at how to market your books online through popular social media sites.

Author Programs we recommend:

Brian Jud – Probably the #1 expert in this field. You can sign up for his services at Book Marketing Works. Brian also offers Book Marketing consultation to any author. If you tell him Laura Dobbins sent you, he will give you a discount but be sure to ask for it before paying.

Association of Publishers for Special Sales – Membership is $89 a year but you get a list of publishers seeking new work. You'll also receive free marketing tips and access to numerous experts in the business like book distributors, buyers and marketers. As a member you're eligible for large discounts regarding anything to do with publishing.

American Authors and Publishers Guild – This is a new membership site that assists independent authors with special sales and publishing needs.

The Cadence Group – Can help you with book packaging needs and sound advice on how to make your book sellable to retail store buyers. Best of all, they'll tell you when not to change a thing.

New Shelves Distribution – Tell them Laura Dobbins sent you. This group specializes in sales to libraries, retailers and specialty shops.

http://www.tckpublishing.com/
TCK – Owned and operated by Tom Corson-Knowles, a respected bestselling author and book marketing expert. His company is an international publisher specializing in ebooks on Amazon Kindle.

Note: Some of these services are expensive with payment often required in advance. We are not their affiliates and will make no profit from your purchase. It should be noted, we only recommend people or services we have used ourselves. Keep in mind THERE ARE NO GUARANTEED BOOK SALES. However, if you are willing to invest some time, money and equity sweat, if you are willing to learn and grow with the industry, you can be a bestseller.

OTHER GOOD AUTHOR SITES we USE OFTEN:

Parapublishing.com – Dan Poynter is an expert on writing, publishing and marketing books. He also has numerous free newsletters including a marketing publication where you can post free books for reviews.

The Kindle Book Review – A site operated by a bestselling author. It is a good forum for authors.

The Author Marketing Club – Great site run by good people and many author tools available.

Digital Book Today – Nice site operated by a veteran book buyer for major retailer. This forum offers marketing tips, promotion opts and much more.

Amazon programs that also help promote your books:

a. **Audio** – ACX is a program offered through Amazon that allows you to produce a digital audiobook version of your book which is integrated with the new Whispersync for Voice on Kindle. The product is a professionally-narrated work.

b. **Look Inside the Book** – this allows customers to skim a portion of your book before deciding on the purchase. Take advantage of this feature by offering enticing text at the start of your work – this means going against the grain of traditional publishing that sets credits, dedications, copyright and table of contents at the front of a book.

c. **Author Central** – This section is like a mini-blog at Amazon. Take advantage of this section with good content, images, interesting tidbits about you and your books. You can also add social media links and book appearance information here.

d. **Amazon Advantage** – This forum works best for small press publishers or book vendors needing distribution and warehousing at reasonable rates.

e. **KDP Select** – This is Amazon's Digital Book Platform and probably the most beneficial for authors. With KDP Select, you can use your book titles, descriptions, categories and keywords to make your book more visible. KDP Select also offers authors free book promotion days and enrollment in the Kindle Lending Library – two programs that give writers visibility and profits.

Amazon has also added three new programs: Kindle Matchbook, Kindle Countdown Deal and Kindle Prime Membership.

KDP and places to list Free Day Promotions:

Amazon Direct Publishing:
https://kdp.amazon.com

Websites with Free Day Submission Tools and Links:

FREE Kindle Book Submission Tool

Over 120 sites to promote your FREE DAYS

Great Author Tools – lots of helpful links

www.rickiwilson.com – Get featured Free

Websites to List Free Day Promos:

http://bit.ly/192zUE

http://bookpraiser.com/submit-book/

http://bit.ly/1pFN5Pj

http://www.fkbooksandtips.com/for-authors/regular-book-posting/

http://www.thekindlebookreview.net/

http://www.pixelofink.com/sfkb/

http://digitalbooktoday.com/12-top-100-submit-your-free-book-to-be-included-on-this-list/

http://worldliterarycafe.com/

http://kindlenationdaily.com/

http://freebooksy.com/

Websites with PROMO opts for Free Day Listings:

https://kindlebookpromos.luckycinda.com – (Our site offers very reasonable prices)

https://www.bookbub.com/partners/pricing - (Your book has to be accepted first)

http://www.booktweetingservice.com/ - (A bit pricey but good service with large audience)

http://www.booksends.com/advertise.php - (Fairly new site but run by a savvy author/marketer)

http://www.bookgorilla.com/advertise - (Fairly new site)

http://digitalbooktoday.com/ - (Great site, good promotion opportunities and run by a book-savvy author and all-around great guy)

http://www.thekindlebookreview.net/ - (Operated by a best-selling author and his team who are very helpful to authors.)

http://www.kboards.com/index.php/topic,11400.0.html – (Slots fill up fast so make sure to coordinate your promo days accordingly.)

Twitter sites to promote Free Days:

@FreeKindleStuff
@FreeReadFeed
@free_kindle
@Freebookdeal
@freebookpromos
@freebooksy
@KindleBookBlast
@KindleDaily
@Kindlbookreview
@digitalBKtoday
@KindleFreeBooks
@kindle_mojo
@Kindlefreebies
@kindlenews
@freebookpromos
@penabook
@Kindlestuff
@KindleEbooksUK
@KindleBookKing
@4FreeKindleBook
@freebookclub1
@ibdbookoftheday
@Booksontheknob
@bookbub
@kindle_free
@freeebooksdaily
@kindlefreebooks
@zilchebooks
@freedailybooks
@free2kindle
@freereadfeed
@pixelofink
@digitalinktoday
@fkbt
@kindlestuff
@free_kindle_fic
@Bookyrnextread

@CheapKindleDly
@DigitalBkToday
@kindlenews
@ebook
@freeebookdeal
@free
@free_kindle
@freebookdude
@4FreeKindleBook
@FreeKindleStuff
@IndAuthorSucess
@IndieKindle
@kindleebooks
@KindleBookKing
@KindleFreeBook
@KindleUpdates
@Kindle_promo
@KindleDaily
@WLCPromotions

Facebook sites to list free days:

https://www.facebook.com/ebookpromos

https://www.facebook.com/AontheC

https://www.facebook.com/iauthor?sk=wall

https://www.facebook.com/IndieKindleWLC

https://www.facebook.com/kindle

https://www.facebook.com/indiebookslist

https://www.facebook.com/ebooksfreefreefree

https://www.facebook.com/mobileread

https://www.facebook.com/freebooktoday

https://www.facebook.com/TheKindleBookReview

https://www.facebook.com/Freebooksy - **(Has a list of other Free Book Listing Sites)**

https://www.facebook.com/FreeBookClub.org

https://www.facebook.com/OneHundredFreeBooks

https://www.facebook.com/DigitalBookToday

https://www.facebook.com/freeebooksdotnet

https://www.facebook.com/IAmAReader

https://www.facebook.com/bookclubbooks

https://www.facebook.com/BookClubGirl

https://www.facebook.com/thereadingroomonline

https://www.facebook.com/BookRiot

https://www.facebook.com/pages/Kindle-Bestseller-Secrets/195560307296759

https://www.facebook.com/groups/270558336379692/

https://www.facebook.com/groups/FreeTodayOnAmazon/

https://www.facebook.com/authormarketingclub

https://www.facebook.com/BookGoodies

https://www.facebook.com/galleycat/app_4949752878

https://www.facebook.com/IndieBookLounge

https://www.facebook.com/IndieKindleWLC

http://www.facebook.com/weloveebooks

http://www.facebook.com/StoryFinds

http://www.facebook.com/pages/UK-Kindle-Book-Lovers/175617412524192

Post here on the day of your Free Day Promotions:

http://snickslist.com/books/place-ad/

http://www.freebookclub.org/kindle-books/book-submissions/

http://addictedtoebooks.com/free

http://www.daily-free-ebooks.com/suggest-free-ebook

http://www.ereaderiq.com/contact/

Kindle Countdown and places to list Promotions:

Sites on how to use Kindle Countdown:

Marketing EasyStreet.
Videos on Youtube:
For US Market
For UK Market

Where to list Kindle Countdown Deals:

USA

Kindle Book Promos – offering free and paid listings for countdown deals.

ereadernewstoday.com – accepting books priced at 99c or lower. Your book will need to have at least 10 reviews with at least a 4 star average rating.

Pixel of Ink - accepts submissions for books priced at 99c or lower.

.efictionfinds.com - accepts submissions for books priced at $2.99 and under. You will need a minimum of 10 reviews, with a 4.0 average rating.

feedyourreader.com - listing books up to $3.99, except on Sundays.

bargainebookhunter.com offering guaranteed listings of 99c books for $10 each and a similar service for books priced up to $5, also costing $10 each. Books must have at least a 4 star rating.

theereadercafe.com - listing 99c books in exchange for a like on Facebook.

Bookbub – One of best promotion sites but expensive depending on your book price and genre. You must be accepted before you are allowed to promote on this site.

worldliterarycafe.com - running '99c Fridays'. It costs $20 to participate.

indiesunlimited.com – offering 'Thrifty Thursdays' for 99c books.

addictedtoebooks.com - accepting free submissions of books costing up to $5.99. Your book must have at least five reviews.

Kindle Nation Daily – offering a range of pay-for services for authors.

digitalbooktoday.com - selling a variety of services for authors.

Thekindlebookreview.net – sells a variety of services for authors. Freebooksy – your book must be priced between 99 cents and $5.

UK

Indie Book Bargains - accepting books priced up to £2.99. Follow instructions.

flurriesofwords UK - offering some cheap paid promotions for bargain books. .

hotukdeals.com - allowing you to list discount books.

bookbargainsuk.com - offering paid promotional opportunities.

FACEBOOK:

Ebookpromos – List your Countdown Deals here.

KindleDailyDeals – Lists all kindle deals. Be sure to follow forum rules.

NookandKindleEbookDeals – Has a form on site for all ebook deals.

KindleCountdownDeals – Open group, make sure to follow forum rules.

Ereader News Today – Lists bargain books.

Twitter:

@EbookCountdown

@KindleDailyDeal

@kindledeals

@freebookpromos

@CrazyKindle

@AllKindleDeals

@KindleDeals

@ShopKindleDeals

Other sites:

<u>Goodreads</u> – You can list your bargain books here but you must be a member of Goodreads

Kindle User Forums – Go to both the US and UK sites – follow forum rules

<u>US</u>

<u>UK</u>

Also don't forget to promote on your own blog and social media sites!

.99 Kindle Deals and places to list Promotions:

Where to list .99 Kindle Promos

Kindle Book Promos – free and paid promotions available.

Bookbub – pricey and you must be approved to list but if you have the right type of book, big sales are possible.

Bargain Booksy – Not as pricey as Bookbub but more costly than other sites. Still, a nice platform for promoting.

Ereader News Today

Many Books

Kindle Nation Daily

The Kindle Book Review

Book Daily

EbookHunter

Book Goodies

Awesomegang

The Independent Author Network

GoodKindles

172

<u>Daily Free ebooks</u> – Don't let the site name fool you, the forum no longer is a free ebook promotion service. Dedicated to books costing 99 cents or less.

Pixel of Ink – Brisk traffic. Be sure to post at least 30 days out.

The following three sites are also high-ranking Alexa blogs but you have to be a member or pay for advertising to take advantage of the premium features available. We have used all three in the past with success. In addition we are members and affiliates of The Author Marketing Club.

The Author Marketing Club – Must be a premium member to use all the great marketing tools, such as book description formatting software for Kindle, which creates an appealing list of your books and converts it to a widget for your blog. This forum also offers free marketing videos and many other helpful applications. The cost is around $100 for one year or you can pay month to month at a higher annual fee.

Note: A basic membership is free. You don't have access to all the cool tools but you still get some great benefits: A forum to list your books for reviews, a tool to submit your free days to several promotion sites and access to many affordable advertising opportunities. We recommend you take advantage of this site.

World Literary Cafe – This is a great site and if you haven't joined, do so. You'll find opportunities to increase your Twitter and Facebook followings. In addition, the Cafe has twitter teams to help get your tweets to a larger audience – especially helpful when running promotions. The site also has book review, blog requests and book marketing forums.

In addition the site hosts 99 cent Fridays and a slew of other marketing opportunities, including some free options.

Book Tweeting Service – This site has a large audience of active book buyers. On one occasion, we used the service for two days and sold 63 books but during another promotion, we used the service for two days and only sold 12 books. Again, there are no guarantees on book sales, but the service is good and the followers are real people looking for books.

BONUS: Here's a UK site that offers low-cost ads on a newsletter that targets English-speaking markets all over the world. They also list INDY bookstores that have online sites as well as Amazon, Kobo and Barnes & Noble. Here's the link: EbookBargainsUK.

Good Twitter Sites:

https://twitter.com/ebooks99cents

https://twitter.com/99KindlePromos

https://twitter.com/99ebooks

https://twitter.com/KindleSwag

https://twitter.com/CrazyKindle

https://twitter.com/99centsale

https://twitter.com/book_tribe

https://twitter.com/AllKindleDeals

List of our other books all available at AMAZON:

Francesca of Lost Nation – Romance Adventure and winner of five literary awards

The Cancer Club - a crazy, sexy, inspirational novel of SURVIVAL
Selected as a top-ten finalist in the Next Best Fiction Author Contest by Hampton Roads Publishing and Hierophant Publishing

Water in the West: The Scary Truth about our most Precious Resource -
An Environmental Essay

The Adventures of Baylard Bear – a Story about being DIFFERENT -
Poynter Global Ebook Honorable Mention – Children's Fiction

Why is Pookie Stinky? For Ages 4 to 7 Years Old (Book One: "Silly" Puppy Series 1) -
Short Picture Book Written in Rhyme

Sell more Ebooks – How to increase sales and Amazon rankings using Kindle Direct Publishing
Poynter Global Ebook First Place Winner – Marketing and Advertising

38418622R00102

Made in the USA
Charleston, SC
04 February 2015